THE GREAT grilled cheese BOOK

THE GREAT grilled cheese BOOK Grown-Up Recipes for a Childhood Classic

ERIC GREENSPAN

Photography by Colin Price

TEN SPEED PRESS
California | New York

Copyright © 2018 by Eric Greenspan
Photographs copyright © 2018 by Colin Price

Published in the United States by Ten Speed Press, an imprint of the Crown
Publishing Group, a division of Penguin Random House LLC, New York.
www.crownpublishing.com
www.tenspeed.com

Ten Speed Press and the Ten Speed Press colophon are registered
trademarks of Penguin Random House LLC.

Library of Congress Cataloging-in-Publication Data is on file with
the publisher.

Hardcover ISBN: 978-0-399-58074-1
eBook ISBN: 978-0-399-58075-8

Printed in China

Interior design by Hope Meng
Cover design by Betsy Stromberg
Food styling by Jeffrey Larsen and Natalie Drobny
Prop styling by Glenn Jenkins

10 9 8 7 6 5 4 3 2 1

First Edition

TO EVERYONE WHO
TAUGHT ME.

TO EVERYONE WHO
SUPPORTED ME.

TO EVERYONE WHO
LEARNED FROM ME.

contents

introduction

I didn't come from a family of world travelers, and I wasn't raised around great food. My only true childhood food memory is of my mother putting a plate on top of thin, crispy grilled cheese sandwiches as they cook. They were delicious, especially the little bits of cheese that oozed out and crisped up on the bottom of the hot pan. But you won't find that technique anywhere in this book.

My love of food developed first with a love of cooking. I started as a short-order cook while attending the University of California, Berkeley. Caffe Med was an open kitchen, and I enjoyed creating simple, delicious food for the customers who quickly became my friends. I knew immediately I wanted to reach people through food. I never thought I would ascend to being a chef recognized for my culinary talents, but I understood that if I was ever going to make a great sandwich, I had to learn how to make a great steak. As someone who had always taken pride in doing my very best work, I knew I needed to learn more, so I set out to study with some of the finest chefs in the world: David Bouley, Alain Ducasse, Ferran Adrià, Joachim Splichal.

The more I learned, the more I grew as a chef. But I never lost sight of the fact that what I loved about food was my love of people. I wanted to take what I learned as a chef and apply it to something everyone could enjoy. So when I opened The Foundry on Melrose in 2007, I chose to eschew the highfalutin cheese plate found in every upstart fine-dining restaurant at the time in favor of an elevated grilled cheese. I wanted the everyman walking by my restaurant to think, "Hey, I like grilled cheese," and wander unbeknownst into a new culinary experience. I took a stinky Taleggio and put it between two slices of the raisin-walnut bread common to a cheese plate but so uncommon to a grilled cheese. I blended dried apricots and capers into a puree and added sun-dried tomato as a nod to the dried fruits and pickles typically found on a cheese plate. For good measure, I added some shredded short-rib beef that happened to be lying around the kitchen, and my signature grilled cheese, The Champ, was born.

What follows builds on the spirit of that sandwich. The recipes take what I've learned about flavor, technique, and texture while working in Michelin-caliber restaurants and puts that knowledge into a package that everyone can relate to—the grilled cheese. From making your own American cheese, jams, and pickles to braising meats and exploring reworked classic dishes, this book takes the grilled cheese sandwich to another level, while keeping true to what it is at its core—delicious.

This book is not meant to be a bible. The recipes are not meant to be law. *The Great Grilled Cheese Book* is instead a point of reference for exploring the many ways this beloved sandwich can be embellished. Each chapter is dedicated to a cheese, so you can easily decide which sandwich to make based on what cheeses are available to you; each recipe makes four sandwiches. In the recipe list at the beginning of each chapter, I've also labeled the recipes as Vegetarian (V), Breakfast (B), Meat and Fish (M), and Sweets (S) to help you tailor your sandwich to your mood.

Play with the recipes. Use them as inspiration for your own creations. Most of all, have as much fun making these grilled cheeses as I have had writing this book. I'm hoping you'll never look at a grilled cheese the same way again.

complexity of recipes

I know what you are thinking: these recipes are pretty involved for making a grilled cheese sandwich! And you're right. I've given you all of the information you need to make every ingredient for each recipe should you choose to do that. If you are looking to make a quick and easy grilled cheese, you can use these recipes as guidelines, substituting, adding, or omitting as you see fit. For me, these grilled cheeses are about having fun, and they should be for you, too.

Keep in mind that many of the components can be made ahead of time. Any of the braised or roasted meats can, and frankly should, be made in advance. Make them for a meal the night before, saving the leftovers for a great next-day grilled cheese. The pickled items and the preserves can be made ahead of time, too, and will keep in the refrigerator for at least two weeks. They can also be used for things other than these sandwiches: cheese and charcuterie boards, garnishes for other dishes, nongrilled sandwiches—have at it!

Sometimes you just want to make a delicious grilled cheese and you are too busy to get as deep into cooking as this book will let you. Many of the more time-consuming components can be replaced with store-bought products, so feel free to buy them. But when you can spend time in the kitchen, I urge you to embrace these recipes and sandwiches for what they are: complex dishes with fun techniques and interesting flavors and textures, all wrapped up in a grilled cheese package.

At the end of the day, don't overthink it. The recipes are meant to be playful, and I don't want that point to be lost. If you've got the time, enjoy the cooking for what it is: an educational and fun experience that ends in a delicious grilled cheese. Happy grilling.

01.
american

I've always said, you've got to know where you're from to know where you're at. This sandwich is where it all started. It is the empty canvas on which all other grilled cheeses are painted. And it's my go-to when my son, Max, needs a quick fix (or I do!). There's something about white bread and American cheese that speaks to the soul of childhood. The key to a Classic is in the details: the bread is grilled to a crisp golden brown and the cheese is melted to gooey, stretchy perfection. And if a little drips out and crisps up around the sides, all the better!

8 slices of homemade American Cheese (page 22)

8 slices white bread

4 tablespoons unsalted butter, for finishing

classic

Line up 4 bread slices on a work surface. Top each slice with 2 cheese slices. Close the sandwiches with the remaining bread slices.

Line a large platter with paper towels. In a skillet over high heat, melt 1 tablespoon of the butter. Turn down the heat to low, add 1 sandwich, and cook, turning once, for 2 to 3 minutes on each side, until browned and crisp on both sides and the cheese is melted. Transfer to the prepared platter to blot the excess grease. Repeat with the remaining butter and sandwiches.

Cut the sandwiches in half, plate, and serve.

There is no better bar food than a great grilled cheese. This sandwich is inspired by the flavors of a German beer hall, where pretzels and mustard rule the day. I've infused the American cheese with beer, which gives it a nuttiness and acidity that cuts the richness of the sandwich. The spice of the mustard and the sweetness of the pretzel bread round out this perfect accompaniment to a pint (or liter!) of beer. If you like, you can swap out the pretzel bread for a German dark rye or pumpernickel.

meltfest

To make the pickles, put the cucumber slices in a large mason jar or other jar with a tight-fitting lid. In a small saucepan, combine the vinegar, kosher salt, sugar, black pepper, bay leaf, mustard seeds, coriander seeds, allspice, red pepper flakes, and clove and bring to a boil over high heat, stirring to dissolve the kosher salt and sugar. Remove from the heat and pour into the jar over the cucumbers. The cucumbers should be submerged in the liquid. Cover tightly and let cool before using.

Line up the bread slices on a work surface. Spread 2 tablespoons of the mustard on each slice. Top 4 of the bread slices with 2 cheese slices, then top the cheese slices with pickles, using about 5 slices for each sandwich. Close the sandwiches with the remaining bread slices, mustard side down.

8 slices of homemade Beer-Infused American Cheese (page 23)

8 slices of pretzel bread

PICKLES

2 large cucumbers, cut crosswise into ¼-inch-thick slices

2 cups cider vinegar

¼ cup kosher salt

2 tablespoons sugar

1 teaspoon freshly ground black pepper

1 bay leaf

1 teaspoon yellow mustard seeds

1 teaspoon coriander seeds

1 teaspoon allspice berries

1 teaspoon red pepper flakes

1 whole clove

½ cup German-style mustard

4 tablespoons unsalted butter, for finishing

Line a large platter with paper towels. In a skillet over high heat, melt 1 tablespoon of the butter. Turn down the heat to low, add 1 sandwich, and cook, turning once, for 2 to 3 minutes on each side, until browned and crisp on both sides and the cheese is melted. Transfer to the prepared platter to blot the excess grease. Repeat with the remaining butter and sandwiches.

Cut the sandwiches in half, plate, and serve.

There is no better cheese for an egg sandwich than American, whether it's "two on a roll" from any corner bodega in New York City or a drive-through Egg McMuffin (admittedly my guilty pleasure). At Greenspan's, we had a ton of requests for breakfast sandwiches, and this became our go-to recipe. The smokiness of the bacon and the peppery notes of the arugula mix with the gooey egg yolk and melted cheese to make for something magical. The sourdough brings a nice acidity, and the Sriracha, which here has been infused into the cheese, adds the perfect heat to bring it all together. If you're short on time, use store-bought American cheese and spread a splash of Sriracha sauce on the bread.

bad moon rising

Preheat the oven to 350°F. Place a large wire rack on a sheet pan. Line a platter with paper towels. Arrange the bacon slices, well spaced, on the rack. (The bacon will cook up crispier on the rack while the fat collects in the pan. This is key to the bacon remaining crisp in a grilled cheese.) Place the bacon in the oven for 15 to 20 minutes, until crisp. Transfer the bacon to the prepared platter to drain.

Heat an 8-inch nonstick skillet over medium heat until hot. Add 2 tablespoons of the oil and heat until it begins to shimmer. Crack 2 of the eggs into the pan and immediately turn down the heat to low. Cook for about 5 minutes, until the whites are set and the yolks are still runny, then transfer the eggs to a large plate. Repeat with

CONTINUED >

8 slices of homemade Sriracha-infused American Cheese (page 23)

8 slices of sourdough bread

8 slices good-quality bacon

8 eggs

½ cup canola oil

4 ounces baby arugula

½ to 1 cup mayonnaise

4 tablespoons unsalted butter, for finishing

the remaining oil and eggs, cooking the eggs two at a time and transferring them to the plate.

Line up the bread slices on a work surface. Spread 1 to 2 table-spoons of the mayonnaise on each slice. Top each bread slice with 1 cheese slice.

Line 1 or 2 large platters with paper towels. In a large skillet over high heat, melt 1 tablespoon of the butter. Add 2 "open-faced" sandwiches and cook for 2 to 3 minutes on low heat, until the cheese is melted and the bread is golden brown. Transfer to the prepared platter to blot the excess grease. Repeat with the remaining butter and sandwiches, cooking 2 sandwiches at a time.

Divide the arugula evenly among 4 of the grilled bread slices, then top each mound of arugula with 2 slices of bacon. Top bacon with 2 fried eggs and follow with the remaining 4 bread slices, popping the yolks with the slightest pressure and letting them ooze into the entire sandwich.

Cut the sandwiches in half, plate, and serve.

cooking basics for a great grilled cheese

Even the simplest grilled cheese requires following some basic rules to make the sandwich great.

First, choose a cheese that melts. I love a good Parmesan or other aged cheese, but it has no place in a grilled cheese. If the cheese doesn't melt—and I mean gooey melt—save it for a great pasta or cheese board. If you choose a good-melting cheese that is difficult to cut into even slices, grate it so you can distribute it evenly.

Second, be careful with your bread selection. These days, the baking world is experiencing a renaissance, so an abundance of incredible breads is out there, many of which make delicious grilled cheese sandwiches. But with the complexity of artisanal bread comes an unevenness (air pockets and holes caused by great yeast and inconsistent sizing) that doesn't necessarily contribute to a great grilled cheese. So be wary. Choose a bread with good tooth to ensure an even golden brown, crisp finish.

Next, use butter. I've heard of using mayonnaise as a spread or vegetable oils for color, but for me, it's not a grilled cheese sandwich if you don't use butter. The butter helps brown the bread and develops a nutty flavor when it toasts in a hot pan that is unsurpassed. Also, don't be afraid to add more butter if you feel the grilled cheese is too dry or not browning properly. A great grilled cheese is health food for the soul—not necessarily the body.

Choose the best pan for the job. I think a heavy cast-iron skillet is perfect. It conducts and holds the heat well, allowing for even cooking without burning the bread or the butter. You can use a griddle, too, but you'll have to soften the butter and spread it on each side of the sandwich before you start cooking. You can also use a grill pan if you like the look of the grill marks. Presentation counts!

Finally, slow it down. A great grilled cheese needs time for the bread to color evenly and the cheese to melt. Don't rush it. Start the sandwich in a hot pan, but quickly lower the temperature and then take the time to crisp the bread and brown it evenly and thoroughly.

When I was filming *Eric Greenspan Is Hungry* for National Geographic, we spent a ton of time in the South with people who are super passionate about food. We were invited into their homes, restaurants, and trailers to try what they've been cooking for generations, and they never ceased to impress. From slow-cooked greens to pimento cheese, the South has a distinct culinary culture that I love to incorporate into my dishes, and I've put some of my favorites into this showstopping sandwich.

south rising

To make the pickles, put the cucumber slices in a mason jar. In a small saucepan, combine the vinegar, salt, sugar, black pepper, bay leaf, mustard seeds, coriander seeds, allspice, red pepper flakes, and clove and bring to a boil over high heat, stirring to dissolve the salt and sugar. Remove from the heat and pour over the cucumbers until they are submerged in the liquid. Cover tightly and let cool before using.

To make the greens, in a saucepan, heat the oil over high heat. Add the greens and cook, stirring constantly, for 2 minutes. Add the vinegar, honey, and hot sauce, stir well, and bring to a boil. Turn down the heat to a gentle simmer and cook uncovered, stirring occasionally, for about 1 hour, until the liquid has evaporated and the greens are tender. If all of the liquid has evaporated and the greens are not yet tender, add water as needed to prevent scorching and continue to cook until tender.

CONTINUED >

8 ounces of homemade Pimento American Cheese (page 23)

8 slices of white bread

BREAD-AND-BUTTER PICKLES

2 large cucumbers, cut crosswise into ¼-inch-thick slices

2 cups cider vinegar

¼ cup kosher salt

¼ cup firmly packed golden brown sugar

1 teaspoon freshly ground black pepper

1 bay leaf

1 teaspoon yellow mustard seeds

1 teaspoon coriander seeds

1 teaspoon allspice berries

1 teaspoon red pepper flakes

1 whole clove

>>

To make the fried chicken, pour the oil to a depth of 2 to 3 inches into a heavy saucepan or deep sauté pan and heat to 350°F on a deep-frying thermometer. Line a large platter with paper towels.

While the oil heats, in a small, shallow bowl, stir together the flour, cayenne pepper, salt, black pepper, and mustard powder. In a medium bowl, combine the chicken tenders and buttermilk and stir to coat evenly. Remove the tenders, letting any excess buttermilk drip back into the bowl, and then dredge them in the flour mixture.

When the oil is ready, working in batches to avoid crowding, lift the tenders one at a time from the flour mixture, shaking off the excess, and slide them into the hot oil. Fry for 4 to 6 minutes, until crisp. Using tongs, transfer to the prepared platter to drain. Repeat with the remaining tenders.

Line up half of the bread slices on a work surface. Spread each slice with ¼ cup of the cheese. Divide the chicken tenders evenly among the slices, then top each sandwich with ¼ cup of the greens. Arrange 3 or 4 pickle slices on each mound of greens. Close the sandwiches with the remaining bread slices.

Line a large platter with paper towels. In a skillet over high heat, melt 1 tablespoon of the butter. Turn down the heat to low, add 1 sandwich, and cook, turning once, for 2 to 3 minutes on each side, until browned and crisp on both sides and the cheese is melted. Transfer to the prepared platter to blot the excess grease. Repeat with the remaining butter and sandwiches.

Cut the sandwiches in half, plate, and serve.

GREENS

¼ cup canola oil

2 bunches collard greens, about 1½ pounds total weight, stemmed and coarsely chopped

1 cup cider vinegar

½ cup honey

¼ cup hot sauce

FRIED CHICKEN

½ gallon canola oil, for deep-frying

1 cup all-purpose flour

1 teaspoon cayenne pepper

1 teaspoon kosher salt

1 teaspoon freshly ground black pepper

1 teaspoon mustard powder

8 ounces chicken tenders

2 cups buttermilk

4 tablespoons unsalted butter, for finishing

I am a great fan of jazz. At my first restaurant, The Foundry on Melrose, we featured live jazz nightly and were lucky to host some of the finest young jazz artists in Los Angeles. My love of jazz led me to a great American culinary tradition, chicken and waffles, a dish that is said to have been created for jazz musicians who worked late and often didn't eat until they stopped playing in the early morning hours. Breakfast? Dinner? It wasn't clear. So the waffles and chicken were combined into a single dish that has been celebrated ever since. Here, I have added a third element, maple American cheese, to make it complete.

night and day

To make the waffles, preheat a waffle iron according to the manufacturer's directions. In a bowl, whisk together the flours, baking powder, baking soda, salt, and sugar. In a separate bowl, whisk together the eggs, buttermilk, and butter. Pour the egg mixture into the flour mixture and whisk until a thick batter forms.

Lightly grease the waffle iron with cooking spray. Ladle one-eighth of the batter onto the center of the grid, close the lid, and cook according to the manufacturer's directions (usually about 5 minutes), until golden brown on both sides. Transfer the waffle to a plate and repeat with the remaining batter. You should have 8 waffles total (if using a standard iron).

To make the fried chicken, pour the oil to a depth of 2 to 3 inches into a heavy saucepan or deep sauté pan and heat to 350°F on a deep-frying thermometer. Line a large platter with paper towels.

CONTINUED >

8 ounces of homemade Maple American Cheese (page 23)

WAFFLES

1 cup all-purpose flour

¼ cup pastry flour

1 teaspoon baking powder

½ teaspoon baking soda

1 teaspoon kosher salt

3 tablespoons sugar

3 large eggs, beaten

2 cups buttermilk, at room temperature

5 tablespoons unsalted butter, melted and cooled

FRIED CHICKEN

½ gallon of canola oil, for deep-frying

1 cup all-purpose flour

1 teaspoon cayenne pepper

1 teaspoon kosher salt

1 teaspoon ground black pepper

1 teaspoon mustard powder

8 ounces chicken tenders

2 cups buttermilk

4 tablespoons unsalted butter, for finishing

Pure maple syrup, for drizzling (optional)

While the oil heats, in a small, shallow bowl, stir together the flour, cayenne pepper, salt, black pepper, and mustard powder. In a medium bowl, combine the chicken tenders and buttermilk and stir to coat evenly. Remove the tenders, letting any excess buttermilk drip back into the bowl, and then dredge them in the flour mixture.

When the oil is ready, working in batches to avoid crowding, lift the tenders one at a time from the flour mixture, shaking off the excess, and slide them into the hot oil. Fry for 4 to 6 minutes, until crisp. Using tongs, transfer to the prepared platter to drain. Repeat with the remaining tenders.

Line up 4 of the waffles on a work surface. Top each waffle with 2 cheese slices, then divide the chicken tenders evenly among the cheese-topped waffles (about 2 tenders per waffle). Close the sandwiches with the remaining waffles.

Large a large platter with paper towels. In a skillet over high heat, melt 1 tablespoon of the butter. Turn down the heat to low and add 1 sandwich. Press down on the top of the sandwich with a spatula to flatten it, then cook, turning once, for 2 to 3 minutes on each side, until browned and crisp on both sides and the cheese is melted. Transfer to the prepared platter to blot the excess grease. Repeat with the remaining butter and sandwiches.

Cut the sandwiches in half, plate, and serve. If you want more maple syrup with your waffle grilled cheese, drizzle some around or on top of the sandwich. If you're worried about getting your hands sticky, a fork and a knife are forgivable.

american cheese

- 8 ounces firm, solid mild Cheddar cheese, finely grated
- 8 ounces firm, solid (low-moisture) mozzarella cheese, finely grated
- 4 tablespoons tapioca flour
- 2 teaspoon kosher salt
- 2 ounces melted unsalted butter
- 1 cup milk

Line a 8½- by 4½- by 2¾-inch loaf pan with plastic wrap. In a food processor, combine the Cheddar, mozzarella, tapioca flour, and kosher salt, and pulse to combine. In a small saucepan, combine the butter and milk and bring to a boil over high heat. Remove from the heat and slowly pour the hot liquid into the cheese, processing until fully melted and smooth. Spoon the mixture into the prepared loaf pan, spreading it evenly. It should fill three-fourths of the loaf pan. Let stand in the refrigerator for several hours, until the cheese sets. Invert the pan to remove the cheese and peel off the plastic wrap. Transfer to a cutting board and cut crosswise into 16 equal slices. This recipe should yield extra cheese. Feel free to use as much as you'd like for a goopy sandwich, or set aside the leftovers. They will last 2 weeks in the refrigerator.

variations

BEER-INFUSED AMERICAN CHEESE

½ cup strong beer

Prepare the American cheese as directed, substituting the beer for ½ cup of the whole milk. Cut into 16 equal slices.

SRIRACHA-INFUSED AMERICAN CHEESE

½ cup Sriracha sauce

Prepare the American cheese as directed, substituting the Sriracha for ½ cup of the whole milk. Cut into 16 equal slices.

PIMENTO AMERICAN CHEESE

¼ teaspoon garlic powder
¼ teaspoon cayenne pepper
¼ teaspoon onion powder
1 jalapeño chile, seeded and minced
1 (4-ounce) jar diced pimientos, drained

To make the cheese, prepare the American cheese as directed, omitting the loaf pan and adding the garlic powder, cayenne pepper, onion powder, jalapeño chile, and pimentos to the food processor with the grated cheeses. Spoon the finished cheese into a jar, let cool, cap, and let stand at room temperature for several hours until set. The cheese should have a spreadable consistency.

MAPLE AMERICAN CHEESE

½ cup pure maple syrup

Prepare the American cheese as directed, substituting the maple syrup for the ½ cup of the whole milk. Cut into 16 equal slices.

02.
mozzarella and provolone

This is my attempt to capture the essence of one of America's greatest sandwiches: the muffuletta from Central Grocery on Decatur Street in New Orleans. I mimic the oily richness of the bread with homemade focaccia, the brine of the olive salad with olives freshened with citrus zest, and the brightness of the *giardiniera* with pickled carrots. The richly spiced tasso ham speaks not only to the smokiness of the cured meats in the original but also reminds me of the Creole culture common in that part of the country. (If you cannot find tasso, other pork cured meats such as mortadella or salami can be substituted.) Finally, the melted mozzarella and provolone may be an improvement on an already perfect sandwich.

muffuletta

To make the focaccia, in a bowl, stir together the flour, salt, sugar, yeast, and rosemary. Add the water and canola oil and, using a wooden spoon, stir until the dough comes together in a rough, shaggy ball. Lightly flour a work surface and turn the dough out onto it. Knead for about 15 minutes, until smooth and elastic, then shape it into a ball.

Oil a large bowl with canola oil, transfer the dough to the bowl, turn the dough to coat evenly with the oil, cover the bowl with a damp kitchen towel, and let the dough rise in a warm spot for 20 minutes. Meanwhile, preheat the oven to 450°F. Oil a 9½- by 13-inch sheet pan with 1 tablespoon of the olive oil.

CONTINUED >

8 ounces provolone cheese, cut into 4 equal slices

8 ounces mozzarella cheese, grated

FOCACCIA

4 cups all-purpose flour

2 teaspoons kosher salt

1 teaspoon sugar

2 teaspoons active dry yeast

1 tablespoon chopped fresh rosemary

2¼ cups water

1 tablespoon canola oil

2 tablespoons olive oil

PICKLED CARROTS

1 bunch baby carrots, trimmed and thinly sliced lengthwise

1 cup red wine vinegar

2 tablespoons kosher salt

1 tablespoon sugar

>>

Punch down the dough and transfer it to the prepared pan. Using your fingers, press the dough evenly over the bottom of the pan. Let rise in a warm spot for an additional 20 minutes. Brush the top with the remaining 1 tablespoon olive oil.

Bake for about 15 minutes, until golden brown. Let cool completely in the pan on a wire rack, then cut into 4 even squares.

To make the carrots, put the carrots in a heatproof bowl. In a small saucepan, combine the vinegar, salt, and sugar and bring to a boil over high heat, stirring to dissolve the salt and sugar. Pour over the carrots and let cool.

To make the olives, in a small bowl, combine all of the ingredients and mix well.

Split each focaccia square in half horizontally. Line up the 4 bottom halves, cut sides down, on a work surface. Top each half with 1 provolone slice, followed by one-fourth each of the olives, carrots, basil, tasso, and mozzarella. Close the sandwiches with the top halves of the focaccia squares, cut sides up.

Large a large platter with paper towels. In a skillet over high heat, melt 1 tablespoon of the butter. Turn down the heat to low and add 1 sandwich. Press down on the top of the sandwich with a spatula to flatten it so it cooks evenly, then cook, turning once, for 2 to 3 minutes on each side, until browned and crisp on both sides and the cheese is melted. Transfer to the prepared platter to blot the excess grease. Repeat with the remaining butter and sandwiches.

Cut the sandwiches in half, plate, and serve.

OLIVES

¼ cup black olives (preferably Niçoise or Kalamata), pitted

¼ cup green olives (preferably Picholine or Castelvetrano), pitted

¼ cup olive oil

1 clove garlic, minced

Grated zest of 1 lemon

Grated zest of 1 orange

Leaves of 1 bunch basil, cut into chiffonade

8 ounces tasso ham, sliced

4 tablespoons unsalted butter, for finishing

This is an update of my original Med, the vegetarian option featured at Greenspan's Grilled Cheese. Its name alludes to the bounty of the Mediterranean; the artichokes, spinach, and red peppers make this point clear. But it's the brightness of the artichokes (fresh or jarred will work) and the sweetness of the jam that, when paired with the creamy provolone and buttery brioche, make its glory come shining through.

the med

To make the jam, in a food processor, combine the peppers, vinegar, and sugar and process until smooth. Transfer to a small, heavy saucepan and bring to a boil over high heat. Turn down the heat to low and cook for about 1 hour until thick, stirring occasionally and being careful not to let it burn. Let cool.

To prepare the artichokes, fill a large bowl with water, squeeze the lemon halves into the water, and add the spent halves. Working with 1 artichoke at a time, pull off the outer leaves until you reach the light yellow leaves. Using a serrated knife, cut off the top one-third of the artichoke and the bottom of the stem. Using a small, sharp knife, trim off the top and sides of the artichoke until you reach the pale green heart, then peel away the fibrous, dark green exterior of the stem. Scoop out the choke with a spoon, cut the trimmed heart lengthwise into eighths, and drop the pieces into the lemon water. Repeat with the remaining artichokes.

CONTINUED >

1 pound provolone cheese, cut into 8 equal slices

8 slices brioche bread

RED PEPPER JAM

4 large red bell peppers, seeded and chopped

1 cup red wine vinegar

1 cup sugar

ARTICHOKES

1 lemon, halved, plus ½ cup fresh juice

4 artichokes

½ cup olive oil

1 tablespoon salt

Leaves of 1 bunch baby spinach

4 tablespoons unsalted butter, for finishing

In a small saucepan, combine the lemon juice, oil, and salt. Drain the artichokes well, add to the pan, and bring slowly to a boil over high heat, stirring to dissolve the salt. Turn down the heat to a gentle simmer and cook for about 3 minutes, until the artichokes are tender when pierced with a knife tip. Strain and let cool.

Line up half of the bread slices on a work surface. Spread ¼ cup of the jam on each slice, top with 1 cheese slice, 8 artichoke pieces, one-fourth of the spinach, and a second cheese slice. Close the sandwiches with the remaining bread slices.

Line a large platter with paper towels. In a skillet over high heat, melt 1 tablespoon of the butter. Turn down the heat to low, add 1 sandwich, and cook, turning once, for 2 to 3 minutes on each side, until browned and crisp on both sides and the cheese is melted. Transfer to the prepared platter to blot the excess grease. Repeat with the remaining butter and sandwiches.

Cut the sandwiches in half, plate, and serve.

Nothing screams summer quite like a caprese salad, with creamy burrata and sweet-tart summer tomatoes matching strength with whole basil leaves and balsamic vinegar. This grilled cheese captures the essence of that great warm-weather dish and elevates it a notch. When burrata is not on the cheese-shop shelf, buffalo mozzarella is a good substitute.

caprese melt

In a small saucepan, bring the vinegar to a boil over high heat. Turn down the heat to low and simmer for about 10 minutes, until reduced to a syrupy consistency. Let cool. (You will need only a small amount of the reduced balsamic; store the remainder in an airtight container in the refrigerator and use on salads, fresh fruits such as peaches, strawberries, and melon, and anywhere you need a sweet jolt of zing.)

Line up half of the bread slices on a work surface. Spread a burrata ball on each slice, then top with 2 tomato slices and 3 basil leaves. Drizzle each sandwich with 1 teaspoon of the reduced balsamic. Close the sandwiches with the remaining bread slices.

Line a large platter with paper towels. In a skillet over high heat, melt 1 tablespoon of the butter. Turn down the heat to low, add 1 sandwich, and cook, turning once, for 2 to 3 minutes on each side, until browned and crisp on both sides and the cheese is melted. Transfer to the prepared platter to blot the excess grease. Repeat with the remaining butter and sandwiches.

Cut the sandwiches in half, plate, and serve.

4 (3-ounce) balls burrata cheese

8 slices sourdough bread

2 cups balsamic vinegar

8 slices heirloom tomato, preferably a mixture of varieties

12 fresh basil leaves

4 tablespoon unsalted butter, for finishing

What goes together better than grilled cheese and tomato? Whether it is an heirloom tomato slice or a dip into tomato soup, these two go together like Bonnie and Clyde. But why stop there? And because we're having a tomato party, the pesto here is lights-out special, too.

tomater

To make the pesto, in a saucepan, combine the tomatoes with water to cover, bring to a boil over medium-high heat, and boil for 5 to 7 minutes, until rehydrated and tender. Drain well and let cool.

In a food processor, combine the cooled tomatoes, basil, garlic, walnuts, and Parmesan and pulse until finely chopped. With the processor running, add the oil in a slow, thin stream and process until the oil is incorporated and the mixture is smooth.

Line up half of the bread slices on a work surface. Top each slice with 1 cheese slice, one-fourth of the pesto, 2 tomato slices, and a second cheese slice. Close the sandwiches with the remaining bread slices.

Line a large platter with paper towels. In a skillet over high heat, melt 1 tablespoon of the butter. Turn down the heat to low, add 1 sandwich, and cook, turning once, for 2 to 3 minutes on each side, until browned and crisp on both sides and the cheese is melted. Transfer to the prepared platter to blot the excess grease. Repeat with the remaining butter and sandwiches.

Cut the sandwiches in half, plate, and serve.

12 ounces mozzarella cheese, grated or cut into 8 slices

8 slices brioche bread

PESTO

1 cup dry-packed sun-dried tomatoes

¼ cup fresh basil leaves

4 cloves garlic, coarsely chopped

¼ cup candied walnuts

¼ cup grated Parmesan cheese

½ cup olive oil

8 slices heirloom tomato

4 tablespoons unsalted butter, for finishing

This grilled cheese is like a visit from your Italian grandmother. The flavors are simple, but everything is made from scratch: the meatballs, the sauce, even the bread. If you are strapped for time and need to buy any or all of these ingredients, by all means do what's necessary to make this recipe. It's the meltiest, most delicious way to enjoy a meatball sandwich.

mulberry street

To make the focaccia, in a bowl, stir together the flour, salt, sugar, yeast, and rosemary. Add the water and canola oil and, using a wooden spoon, stir until the dough comes together in a rough, shaggy ball. Lightly flour a work surface and turn the dough out onto it. Knead for about 15 minutes, until smooth and elastic, then shape into a ball.

Oil a large bowl with canola oil, transfer the dough to the bowl, turn the dough to coat evenly with the oil, cover the bowl with a damp kitchen towel, and let the dough rise in a warm spot for 20 minutes. Meanwhile, preheat the oven to 450°F. Oil a 9½- by 13-inch sheet pan with 1 tablespoon of the olive oil.

Punch down the dough and transfer it to the prepared pan. Using your fingers, press the dough evenly over the bottom of the pan. Let rise in a warm spot for an additional 20 minutes. Brush the top with the remaining 1 tablespoon olive oil.

Bake for about 15 minutes, until golden brown. Let cool completely in the pan on a wire rack, then cut into 4 even squares.

8 ounces fresh mozzarella cheese, cut into 8 slices

FOCACCIA

4 cups all-purpose flour

2 teaspoons kosher salt

1 teaspoon sugar

2 teaspoons active dry yeast

1 tablespoon chopped fresh rosemary

2¼ cups water

1 tablespoon canola oil

2 tablespoons olive oil

SPICY TOMATO SAUCE

½ cup olive oil

3 cloves garlic, minced

1 shallot, minced

¾ teaspoon red pepper flakes

1 28-ounce can San Marzano or other good-quality tomatoes, with juices

Kosher salt and freshly ground black pepper to taste

To make the tomato sauce, in a saucepan, heat the oil over high heat. Add the garlic, shallot, and red pepper flakes and cook, stirring, for 7 to 10 minutes, until tender and translucent. Add the tomatoes and their juices and bring to a boil, breaking up the tomatoes with a wooden spoon. Lower the heat to a gentle simmer and cook, stirring occasionally, for about 1¼ hours, until the tomatoes are reduced to a sauce-like consistency. Season with salt and pepper.

While the sauce cooks, make the meatballs. Preheat the oven to 350°F. In a bowl, combine all of the ingredients and mix well. Divide the meat mixture into 8 equal portions, shape each portion into a ball, and arrange them on a sheet pan. Bake for 5 minutes to set. Remove from the oven.

When the sauce is ready, add the meatballs and cook for 5 to 7 minutes, until cooked through. Remove the pan from the heat, then scoop out the meatballs and place them on a plate.

Split each focaccia square in half horizontally. Line up the 4 bottom halves, cut sides down, on a work surface. Slather ¼ cup of the tomato sauce on each half. Top with 2 mozzarella slices and then 2 meatballs, pressing down lightly on the meatballs. Cover with the top halves of the focaccia squares, cut sides up.

Large a large platter with paper towels. In a skillet over high heat, melt 1 tablespoon of the butter. Turn down the heat to low and add 1 sandwich. Press down on the top of the sandwich with a spatula to flatten it so it cooks evenly, then cook, turning once, for 3 to 4 minutes on each side, until browned and crisp on both sides and the cheese is melted. Transfer to the prepared platter to blot the excess grease. Repeat with the remaining butter and sandwiches.

Cut the sandwiches in half, plate, and serve.

MEATBALLS

4 ounces ground pork

4 ounces ground beef

1 egg

6 tablespoons olive oil

1 ounce fine dried bread crumbs

1 tablespoon chopped fresh oregano

4 tablespoons unsalted butter, for finishing

03.
cheddar

Cheddar, tomatoes, onions—classic, right? This recipe highlights how to make an extraordinary grilled cheese out of ordinary ingredients by maximizing your ingredients in three ways: heightening their flavor, manipulating their texture, and sourcing them well. Slow roasting the tomatoes intensifies their flavor, while preparing the onions two ways highlights the versatility of a humble ingredient and creates two distinctive textures. But the key to this sandwich is sourcing a great Cheddar. For me—and I'm in good company—there is no finer American-made Cheddar than Cabot Clothbound Cheddar by Jasper Hill Farm in Vermont. It is aged for nine to fourteen months, developing a sharp acidity and deep caramel nuttiness that pairs perfectly with the sweet tang of the tomatoes and the bite of the onions in this sandwich. If your cheese store doesn't stock it, any sharp Cheddar can be substituted.

the new standard

To make the tomatoes, preheat the oven to 300°F. In a bowl, combine the tomatoes, salt, and oil and stir to coat the tomatoes evenly. Spread the tomatoes in a single layer on a sheet pan and roast for 45 minutes to 1 hour, until the skins split and wrinkle and the tomatoes soften but are still intact. Remove from the oven.

To make the marmalade, combine all of the ingredients in a small, heavy saucepan and bring to a boil over medium-high heat, stirring to dissolve the sugar. Turn down the heat to low and simmer gently, stirring occasionally, for about 30 minutes, until the onions

12 ounces Jasper Hill Farm Cabot Clothbound Cheddar cheese, cut into 8 equal slices or grated

8 slices pumpernickel bread

OVEN-DRIED TOMATOES

1 pint mixed heirloom cherry tomatoes

½ tablespoon kosher salt

¼ cup olive oil

RED ONION MARMALADE

2 red onions, thinly sliced

¼ cup red wine vinegar

¼ cup sugar

FRIED ONION

Canola or other neutral oil, for deep-frying

1 cup buttermilk

½ red onion, thinly sliced

1 cup all-purpose flour

1 raw red onion, thinly sliced

4 tablespoons unsalted butter, for finishing

are tender and the liquid has reduced by two-thirds. Remove from the heat, let cool slightly, then transfer to a food processor and process until smooth.

To make the fried onion, pour the oil to a depth of 1 to 2 inches into a heavy saucepan or deep sauté pan and heat to 350°F on a deep-frying thermometer. Line a plate with paper towels.

While the oil heats, pour the buttermilk into a small bowl and spread the flour in a second small bowl. Dip the onion slices in the buttermilk, allowing the excess to drain back into the bowl, and then dredge them in the flour, shaking off the excess. Slide the onions into the hot oil and fry for 2 to 3 minutes, until golden brown and crisp. Using a slotted spoon, transfer to the prepared plate to drain.

Line up half of the bread slices on a work surface. Spread 2 tablespoons of the marmalade on each slice, then top with 1 cheese slice, one-fourth of the tomatoes, a second cheese slice, and finish with one-fourth each of the fried onion and raw onion. Close the sandwiches with the remaining bread slices.

Large a large platter with paper towels. In a skillet over high heat, melt 1 tablespoon of the butter. Turn down the heat to low, add 1 sandwich, and cook, turning once, for 2 to 3 minutes on each side, until browned and crisp on both sides and the cheese is melted. Transfer to the prepared platter to blot the excess grease. Repeat with the remaining butter and sandwiches.

Cut the sandwiches in half, plate, and serve.

jams

Using a jam is a great way to class up your grilled cheese. If the acidity and crunch of a pickle is flavor's yin, the sweetness and smooth texture of a great jam is its yang.

And fortunately, making a jam could not be simpler. Combine fruit and sugar, sometimes with a splash of water, and cook slowly until the liquid evaporates and the fruit breaks down. The perfect addition to a great grilled cheese is that easy.

Jams can take time to make, however. It's important not to cook the fruit too quickly or you might burn the sugars, and as the jam thickens, you must turn down the heat and stay close by, stirring constantly. Take your time and you will be rewarded.

The jam recipes in this book (see pages 29 and 79) often yield more than you will need for four sandwiches (sometimes you need to make a larger quantity just to ensure it will whirl up smoothly in a blender), but you will find it easy to use up the extra. You can make jams ahead of time and in bulk, too, as they will keep in an airtight container in the refrigerator for up to 2 weeks—or even longer if you use sterilized jars and process them in a hot-water bath.

Don't relegate jam to only sweet sandwiches. It can be a good balance to a savory sandwich that contains a salty cheese or cured meat. You can also add a little vinegar to your sweet jam to make it into a chutney that will add punch to the richest grilled cheese.

Finally, don't be bashful about coming up with alternative jams. For example, vegetables like golden beets, carrots, red peppers, and onions all have a natural sweetness that lend themselves to the jam pot.

One of my favorite grilled cheeses is a tuna melt. My version is particularly good because it cooks the star, tuna, slowly and properly. I named this sandwich after Monterey Bay, California's best source of albacore tuna. And the playful combination of cucumber and grapes? Well, you can thank my wife, Jamie, for that inspired culinary contribution.

monterey melt

To poach the tuna, in a small saucepan, combine the oil, garlic, and bay leaf over medium heat, bring to a simmer, and simmer for about 20 minutes until the garlic is soft. Remove from the heat and strain through a fine-mesh sieve into a medium saucepan. Discard the bay leaf and set the garlic aside.

Season the tuna with salt, then immerse it in the hot oil. Let stand for about 20 minutes, until the tuna is cooked through and flakes easy. Drain the tuna, transfer to a bowl, and break the chunks into flakes.

To make the lemon sauce, combine all of the ingredients in a blender and process until smooth. Add half of the sauce to the tuna and mix with a fork to make a tuna salad. Let cool.

Line up half of the bread slices on a work surface. Spread 2 tablespoons of the remaining lemon sauce on each slice, then top with 1 cheese slice and with one-fourth of the tuna salad.

CONTINUED >

12 ounces sharp Cheddar cheese, cut into 8 equal slices or grated

8 slices wheat bread

POACHED TUNA

8 cups olive oil

1 cup garlic cloves

1 bay leaf

1 pound sushi-grade albacore tuna fillet, cut into 2-inch chunks

1 teaspoon kosher salt

LEMON SAUCE

2 cups mayonnaise

½ cup fresh lemon juice

reserved garlic from tuna

1 cucumber, thinly sliced

1 cup seedless red grapes, halved

4 tablespoons unsalted butter, for finishing

Arrange one-fourth of the cucumber slices and then one-fourth of the grapes on the tuna and finish with a second slice of cheese. Close the sandwiches with the remaining bread slices.

Line a large platter with paper towels. In a skillet over high heat, melt 1 tablespoon of the butter. Turn down the heat to low, add 1 sandwich, and cook, turning once, for 2 to 3 minutes on each side, until browned and crisp on both sides and the cheese is melted. Transfer to the prepared platter to blot the excess grease. Repeat with the remaining butter and sandwiches.

Cut the sandwiches in half, plate, and serve.

As mentioned in the introduction, my first real cooking job was in college as a short-order cook at Caffe Mediterraneum on Telegraph Avenue in Berkeley, California. Every Sunday morning without fail, three of my good friends, Ali, Maher, and Sami, would walk up to the kitchen, flash me a wicked smile, and place their order: three patty melts. This was followed by an immediate scowl and expletive from yours truly. You see, Caffe Med had a griddle far too small for the amount of breakfast we served, so while I appreciated their devotion, it always seemed to signal the beginning of the hardest part of my shift. I still have a deep love for those guys, and I love me a good patty melt—it's the love child of a burger and a grilled cheese after all!

patty melt

To make the patties, in a bowl, combine the beef, salt, and pepper and mix well. Divide the meat into 4 equal portions and shape each portion into a patty.

In a large skillet, warm the oil over high heat. Add the patties and sear, turning once, for about 3 minutes on each side, until lightly charred on both sides. The patties should be rare. Transfer to a plate and let rest.

To make the onions, return the skillet to medium heat and melt the butter. Add the onions and cook, stirring occasionally, for about 15 minutes, until they begin to caramelize in the butter

CONTINUED >

12 ounces sharp Cheddar cheese, cut into 8 equal slices or grated

8 slices rye bread

PATTIES

1½ pounds ground beef (80 percent lean)

1 tablespoon kosher salt

1 teaspoon coarsely ground black pepper

¼ cup canola oil

CARAMELIZED ONIONS

4 tablespoons unsalted butter

2 white onions, thinly sliced

4 tablespoons unsalted butter, for finishing

and remaining beef fat. Turn down the heat to low and cook slowly, stirring occasionally, for about 10 minutes, until translucent and richly caramelized. Remove from the heat.

Line up half of the bread slices on a work surface. Top each slice with 1 cheese slice, a seared patty, one-fourth of the onions, and a second slice of cheese. Close the sandwiches with the remaining bread slices.

Line a large platter with paper towels. In a skillet over high heat, melt 1 tablespoon of the butter. Turn down the heat to low, add 1 sandwich, and cook, turning once, for 2 to 3 minutes on each side, until browned and crisp on both sides and the cheese is melted. Transfer to the prepared platter to blot the excess grease. Repeat with the remaining butter and sandwiches.

Cut the sandwiches in half, plate, and serve.

The greatness of this sandwich depends on its simplicity, so it requires the finest ingredients to impress. When shopping for the ham, if possible, choose Father's Country Hams in Bremen, Kentucky, where the family has been curing its own hams since 1945 on a farm it has owned since 1840. For the cheese, if you can get your hands on it, buy cave-aged Grafton Village Cheddar from Vermont. Great ingredients and a classic flavor combination are sometimes all you need for an extraordinary sandwich.

the simple life

To roast the broccoli, preheat the oven to 350°F. In a bowl, combine the broccoli, oil, and garlic and toss to coat the broccoli evenly. Transfer to a baking dish and roast for about 1 hour, until the broccoli and garlic are tender and slightly charred. Let cool to room temperature. Use a fork to crush the broccoli and garlic, then mix the garlic and oil with the broccoli until fully incorporated.

Line up half of the bread slices on a work surface. Top each slice with 2 cheese slices, one-fourth of the broccoli, 2 ham slices, and a third cheese slice. Close the sandwiches with the remaining bread slices.

Line a large platter with paper towels. In a skillet over high heat, melt 1 tablespoon of the butter. Turn down the heat to low, add 1 sandwich, and cook, turning once, for 2 to 3 minutes on each side, until browned and crisp on both sides and the cheese is melted. Transfer to the prepared platter to blot the excess grease. Repeat with the remaining butter and sandwiches.

Cut the sandwiches in half, plate, and serve.

12 ounces sharp Cheddar cheese, cut into 12 equal slices or grated

8 slices potato bread

OVEN-ROASTED BROCCOLI

2 crowns broccoli, cut into florets

½ cup olive oil

2 cloves garlic

8 ounces country ham, cut into 8 equal slices

4 tablespoons butter, for finishing

The Johnny Apple Cheese was the best seller at Greenspan's Grilled Cheese on Melrose. We started with the familiar flavors of a Jewish deli, and we added earthy Cheddar, the bite of chutney, and crisp green apple. The result is a balanced, meaty, flavorful masterpiece that attacks every taste node on your palate.

johnny apple cheese

To make the chutney, in a saucepan, melt 2 tablespoons of the butter over high heat until it foams. Add the mustard seeds and toast, stirring, for 1 minute. Set aside 12 apple slices, then add the remaining apple slices and the onion to the pan and cook, stirring often, for about 15 minutes, until the apples and onion are tender. Add the cider, vinegar, honey, and mustard, stir well, and cook over low heat, stirring occasionally, for about 30 minutes, until the liquid has evaporated. Let cool slightly, transfer to a blender, and process until nearly smooth. Let cool.

Line up half of the bread slices on a work surface. Top each slice with 2 cheese slices, one-fourth of the pastrami, a dollop of the chutney, and 3 apple slices. Close the sandwiches with the remaining bread slices.

Line a large platter with paper towels. In a skillet over high heat, melt 1 tablespoon of the butter. Turn down the heat to low, add 1 sandwich, and cook, turning once, for 2 to 3 minutes on each side, until browned and crisp on both sides and the cheese is melted. Transfer to the prepared platter to blot the excess grease. Repeat with the remaining butter and sandwiches.

Cut the sandwiches in half, plate, and serve.

12 ounces sharp Cheddar cheese, cut into 8 equal slices or grated

8 slices extra-sour sourdough bread

APPLE MUSTARD CHUTNEY

1 cup unsalted butter

½ cup yellow mustard seeds

5 Granny Smith apples, halved and thinly sliced

1 yellow onion, thinly sliced

½ cup apple cider

½ cup cider vinegar

2 tablespoons honey

2 tablespoons Dijon mustard

1 pound pastrami, thinly sliced

4 tablespoons unsalted butter, for finishing

04.
blue

I like nothing more than to take a classic dish and flip it inside out. This grilled cheese, where I've taken all of the flavors of a Cobb salad and turned them into a rich sandwich, is a good example of this. The avocado dice becomes a spread; the tomatoes switch to a chutney; the romaine gets reworked with a char, replacing the smoke of the bacon so it's not even missed; and the egg remains hard boiled. The corn? It's in the bread. This is a Cobb like you've never had before—but should.

the cobb

To make the cornbread, preheat the oven to 350°F. Spray two 8½- by 4½-inch loaf pans with cooking spray and dust with cornmeal, tapping out the excess. In a large bowl, stir together the flour, cornmeal, sugar, baking powder, baking soda, and salt. In a small bowl, whisk together the eggs, butter, and buttermilk just until blended. Add the egg mixture to the flour mixture and stir just until combined.

Pour the batter into the prepared pans and bake for about 1 hour, until a toothpick inserted in the center comes out clean. Let cool in the pans on a wire rack for at least 20 minutes, then turn out of the pans onto the rack and let cool. Cut lengthwise into 8 even slices.

While the cornbread bakes and cools, make the chutney. Combine all of the ingredients in a small saucepan over medium-high heat and bring to a simmer, stirring to dissolve the sugar. Turn down the heat to low and cook, stirring occasionally, for about 30 minutes, until the liquid has evaporated. Let cool.

CONTINUED >

1 pound blue cheese, crumbled

CORNBREAD

3 cups all-purpose flour

3 cups yellow cornmeal

1½ cups sugar

1 teaspoon baking powder

½ teaspoon baking soda

1 teaspoon kosher salt

4 eggs

1 cup unsalted butter, melted and cooled

2 cups buttermilk

TOMATO CHUTNEY

4 tomatoes, cored and quartered

½ cup sugar

1 teaspoon kosher salt

½ cup cider vinegar

CRUSHED AVOCADO

2 avocados, halved, pitted, and peeled

¼ cup olive oil

>>

To cook the eggs, place them in a small saucepan, add water to cover, and place over medium heat. Bring to gentle boil, remove from the heat, and let the eggs sit in the water for 17 minutes. Remove the eggs from the water, let cool, peel, and thinly slice crosswise.

To make the crushed avocado, put the avocado halves in a bowl. As you slowly drizzle the olive oil into the bowl, use a fork to mix the oil with the avocado to create a chunky puree.

To make the romaine, heat a cast-iron skillet over high heat. Add the canola oil and when the oil is hot, add the romaine and turn as needed until charred on all sides. Turn down the heat to low and cook, turning as needed, for about 5 minutes, or until the lettuce is tender. Transfer the lettuce to a cutting board, cut away the core, and cut the head lengthwise into quarters.

Line up half of the bread slices on a work surface. Spread ¼ cup of the chutney on each slice, then top with 2 ounces (6 to 7 tablespoons) of the cheese and one-fourth of the avocado. Fold a quarter of the romaine on top, add another 2 ounces of the cheese, and finish with one-fourth of the egg slices. Close the sandwiches with the remaining bread slices.

Line a large platter with paper towels. In a skillet over high heat, melt 1 tablespoon of the butter. Turn down the heat to low, add 1 sandwich, and cook, turning once, for 2 to 3 minutes on each side, until browned and crisp on both sides and the cheese is melted. Transfer to the prepared platter to blot the excess grease. Repeat with the remaining butter and sandwiches.

Cut the sandwiches in half, plate, and serve.

CHARRED ROMAINE

¼ cup canola oil

1 head romaine lettuce

4 eggs

4 tablespoons unsalted butter, for finishing

I call this one The Good and Proper because it has everything it needs to be a flavor party—spicy, briny pepperoncini, the sharp bite of the blue cheese and red onion, fresh tomato, and smoky-sweet candied bacon. To complement the smokiness of the bacon, I use Smokey Blue from Rogue Creamery in Oregon. It is cold smoked over hazelnut shells, which imparts sweet and earthy tones to an already rich blue cheese. It eats like candied bacon, so why not pair it with candied bacon? If you cannot find Rogue Creamery blue, another good-quality smoked blue will do.

the good and proper

To cook the bacon, preheat the oven to 350°F. Place a large wire rack on a sheet pan. Line a platter with paper towels. Arrange the bacon slices, well spaced, on the rack. Brush each slice with maple syrup and then sprinkle with the pepper, dividing it evenly. (The bacon will cook up crispier on the rack while the fat collects in the pan. This is key to the bacon remaining crisp in a grilled cheese.) Place the bacon in the oven for 15 to 20 minutes, until crisp. Transfer the bacon to the prepared platter to drain.

Line up half of the bread slices on a work surface. Top each slice with 2 ounces (6 to 7 tablespoons) of the cheese, 2 tomato slices, one-fourth of the onion, 2 bacon slices, and one-fourth of the pepperoncini, then finish with another 2 ounces of the cheese. Close the sandwiches with the remaining bread slices.

CONTINUED >

1 pound Rogue Creamery Smokey Blue cheese

8 slices white bread

CANDIED BACON

8 slices good quality bacon

¼ cup pure maple syrup

1 tablespoon coarsely cracked black pepper

2 tomatoes, preferably heirloom, cut into 8 slices

1 red onion, thinly sliced

1 cup chopped pepperoncini

4 tablespoons unsalted butter, for finishing

Line a large platter with paper towels. In a skillet over high heat, melt 1 tablespoon of the butter. Turn down the heat to low, add 1 sandwich, and cook, turning once, for 2 to 3 minutes on each side, until browned and crisp on both sides and the cheese is melted. Transfer to the prepared platter to blot the excess grease. Repeat with the remaining butter and sandwiches.

Cut the sandwiches in half, plate, and serve.

This grilled cheese is inspired by one of my favorite tapas, a date stuffed with blue cheese and wrapped in bacon. The fatty and salty ham, the sweet date, and the acidity and sharpness of the blue cheese wake up every taste sensation in preparation for the great meal to come. You will end up with more marmalade than you need for the sandwiches, but it will keep in the refrigerator for a couple of weeks and is delicious on nearly everything.

frenchie

To make the marmalade, in a small saucepan, combine the dates and pomegranate juice and bring to a simmer over medium heat. Cook, stirring occasionally, for about 10 minutes, until the dates are soft and tender. Remove from the heat, let cool slightly, then transfer to a food processor and process until a chunky puree forms.

Split each baguette quarter in half horizontally. Line up the bottom halves, cut sides down, on a work surface. Spread ¼ cup of the marmalade on each bottom half, top with 2 ounces of the cheese (6 to 7 tablespoons), then 2 ham slices, and finally another 2 ounces of the cheese. Close the sandwiches with the baguette tops, cut sides up.

Line a large platter with paper towels. In a skillet over high heat, melt 1 tablespoon of the butter. Turn down the heat to low, add 1 sandwich, and cook, turning once, for 2 to 3 minutes on each side, until browned and crisp on both sides and the cheese is melted. Transfer to the prepared platter to blot the excess grease. Repeat with the remaining butter and sandwiches.

Cut the sandwiches in half, plate, and serve.

1 pound blue cheese, crumbled

1 baguette, cut crosswise into quarters

DATE MARMALADE

8 ounces pitted dates

1 cup pomegranate juice

8 thin slices dry-cured ham (such as prosciutto or serrano)

4 tablespoons unsalted butter, for finishing

This sandwich brings together two American favorites: grilled cheese and hot wings. Although blue cheese dressing is easily replicated in the sandwich by using blue cheese, it's the carrot-celery slaw and the hot sauce–laden fried chicken that make the Buffalo Blue sing. It's a familiar taste done in a totally different way! If you like, trade out Frank's RedHot for your preferred hot sauce.

buffalo blue

To make the fried chicken, pour the oil to a depth of 2 to 3 inches into a heavy saucepan or deep sauté pan and heat to 350°F on a deep-frying thermometer. Line a large platter with paper towels.

While the oil heats, in a small, shallow bowl, stir together the flour, cayenne pepper, salt, black pepper, and mustard powder. In a medium bowl, combine the chicken tenders and buttermilk and stir to coat evenly. Remove the tenders, letting any excess buttermilk drip back into the bowl, and then dredge them in the flour mixture.

When the oil is ready, working in batches to avoid crowding, lift the tenders one at a time from the flour mixture, shaking off the excess, and slide them into the hot oil. Fry for 4 to 6 minutes, until crisp. Using tongs, transfer to the prepared platter to drain. Repeat with the remaining tenders. Transfer the fried tenders to a bowl, add the hot sauce, and toss to coat evenly. Cut each tender in half.

To make the slaw, in a large bowl, combine all of the ingredients and mix well.

1 pound blue cheese, crumbled

8 slices rye bread

FRIED CHICKEN

½ gallon of canola oil, for deep-frying

1 cup all-purpose flour

1 teaspoon cayenne pepper

1 teaspoon kosher salt

1 teaspoon freshly ground black pepper

1 teaspoon mustard powder

8 ounces chicken tenders

2 cups buttermilk

½ cup Frank's RedHot hot sauce

CARROT-CELERY SLAW

2 large carrots, peeled and grated

4 celery stalks, grated

1 celery root, peeled and grated

¼ cup mayonnaise

2 tablespoons cider vinegar

1 tablespoon sugar

1 tablespoon kosher salt

4 tablespoons unsalted butter, for finishing

Line up half of the bread slices on a work surface. Top each slice with 2 ounces (6 to 7 tablespoons) of the cheese, one-fourth each of the chicken and slaw, and then another 2 ounces of the cheese. Close the sandwiches with the remaining bread slices.

Line a large platter with paper towels. In a skillet over high heat, melt 1 tablespoon of the butter. Turn down the heat to low, add 1 sandwich, and cook, turning once, for 2 to 3 minutes on each side, until browned and crisp on both sides and the cheese is melted. Transfer to the prepared platter to blot the excess grease. Repeat with the remaining butter and sandwiches.

Cut the sandwiches in half, plate, and serve.

textures

A classic grilled cheese is a study in simplicity. Melted cheese is great, but any grilled cheese will fall flat without crisp bread. Beyond that, I've always found that adding textures to a grilled cheese makes the ordinary extraordinary.

We eat with all of our senses: We smell the toasting bread, see the melting cheese, hear the sizzling butter, and taste the flavors with each bite. But it's the textures that allow us to experience touch, our fifth and final sense.

A great way to introduce texture is by adding something crispy. Whether it be fried chicken, fried chickpeas, or crisp onions, that snap always breaks up the monotony of melted cheese. Similarly, something crunchy—raw or pickled vegetables, a fresh slaw, toasted nuts—can bring a layer of texture that keeps each bite interesting. Salad greens, like spinach or arugula, also add a pop of freshness that keeps the party going.

For me, good use of textures is especially important to keeping the eating experience interesting. After the first couple of bites, a grilled cheese can become boring. The addition of textures ensures every bite is a new adventure.

The steakhouse dinner is the quintessential American dining experience. This grilled cheese is founded on blue cheese being the preferred complement to a juicy steak. The rest are merely the traditional side dishes reworked: crispy onions for onion rings, fresh spinach for creamed, and, of course, potato bread stands in for the copious potatoes offered in a steakhouse, from hash browns to double baked.

steakhouse

To make the fried onion, pour the oil to a depth of 1 to 2 inches into a heavy saucepan or deep sauté pan and heat to 350°F on a deep-frying thermometer. Line a plate with paper towels.

While the oil heats, pour the buttermilk into a small bowl. In a second small bowl, stir together the flour, paprika, chili powder, and black pepper. When the oil is ready, dip the onion slices into the buttermilk, allowing the excess to drain back into the bowl, and then dredge them in the flour mixture, shaking off the excess. Slide the onions into the hot oil and fry for 2 to 3 minutes, until golden brown and crisp. Using a slotted spoon, transfer to the prepared plate to drain.

To make the steak, preheat a large cast-iron skillet over high heat. Add the butter and heat until foamy and browned. Add the garlic and thyme and cook, stirring occasionally, for about 2 minutes, until their flavor has infused the butter. Add the steak and cook,

CONTINUED >

1 pound blue cheese, crumbled

8 slices potato bread

FRIED ONION

½ gallon canola oil, for deep-frying

1 cup buttermilk

1 cup all-purpose flour

1 teaspoon paprika

1 teaspoon chili powder

1 teaspoon freshly ground black pepper

½ red onion, thinly sliced

NEW YORK STEAK

6 tablespoons unsalted butter, at room temperature

2 cloves garlic, crushed

2 thyme sprigs

8 ounces New York steak, cut into 1-inch cubes

Leaves of 1 bunch spinach (16 to 20 leaves)

4 tablespoons unsalted butter, for finishing

turning as needed, for about 10 minutes, until browned on all sides and still medium rare in the center. Using a slotted spoon, transfer to a plate and let rest.

Line up half of the bread slices on a work surface. Top each slice with 2 ounces (6 to 7 tablespoons) of the cheese, one-fourth of the steak, 4 or 5 spinach leaves, an additional 2 ounces of the cheese, and finish with one-fourth of the onion. Close the sandwiches with the remaining bread slices.

Line a large platter with paper towels. In a skillet over high heat, melt 1 tablespoon of the butter. Turn down the heat to low, add 1 sandwich, and cook, turning once, for 2 to 3 minutes on each side, until browned and crisp on both sides and the cheese is melted. Transfer to the prepared platter to blot the excess grease. Repeat with the remaining butter and sandwiches.

Cut the sandwiches in half, plate, and serve.

05.
bloomy and washed rinds

ICHABOD CRANE

*Camembert on potato bread with
pumpkin chutney and pumpkin seed oil (V)*..72

PRIME TIME

*Brie on sourdough with beet-horseradish mayonnaise,
caramelized onion, roast beef, and beet slices (M)*.............................75

MORNING MONTE

*Triple cream on French toast with fried chicken,
bacon, and strawberry jam (B, M, S)*...79

THE CHAMP

*Taleggio on raisin-walnut bread with apricot-caper spread,
sun-dried tomatoes, arugula, and short ribs (M)*..................................83

CHERRY CHEESE BALL

*Camembert on challah with sour cherry marmalade
and pistachios (V, S)*...85

This sandwich is named for "The Legend of Sleepy Hollow," one of my favorite fall stories. I think of it every time I drive through upstate New York and New England, where the leaves change color and the entire countryside looks like a painting. This sandwich highlights those regions, and in doing so, brings autumn to mind.

Some of America's best pumpkins come from Small Ones Farm in South Amherst, Massachusetts. And if you can find it, I recommend the Hudson Valley Camembert from Old Chatham Sheepherding Company in Old Chatham, New York. Its creamy nuttiness is the perfect balance to the brightness of the pumpkin chutney and the sweetness of the roast pumpkin. Otherwise, any top-notch Camembert will do.

ichabod crane

To make the chutney, preheat the oven to 400°F. Cut the pumpkins in half through the stem end and scoop out the seeds and any fibers with a spoon. Rinse the seeds and set aside. Place the pumpkin halves, cut sides up, on a large sheet pan and fill the cavities with the butter, garlic, star anise, cinnamon, and thyme, dividing them evenly.

Roast for about 1 hour, until tender when pierced with a knife. Let the pumpkins cool until they can be handled, then peel and cut into ½-inch cubes, discarding the seasonings. Leave the oven on.

Coat the reserved pumpkin seeds with the pumpkin seed oil, spread the seeds on a sheet pan, and toast in the oven for about 10 minutes, until crunchy. Pour onto a plate and set aside.

3 (6-ounce) wheels Old Chatham Sheepherding Hudson Valley Camembert cheese, rind removed

8 slices potato bread

PUMPKIN CHUTNEY

2 sugar pumpkins, 6 to 10 pounds each

4 tablespoons unsalted butter, melted

2 cloves, garlic, halved

4 star anise pods,

2 cinnamon stick, broken in half

4 thyme sprigs

2 tablespoons pumpkin seed oil

2 tablespoons canola oil

1 red onion, diced

¼ cup golden raisins

¼ cup dried sour cherries

¼ cup dried cranberries

1 cup cider vinegar

Pumpkin seed oil, for drizzling

4 tablespoons unsalted butter, for finishing

In a sauté pan, heat the canola oil over high heat. Add the onion and cook, stirring occasionally, for about 10 minutes, until tender and lightly caramelized. Remove from the heat. Meanwhile, in a small saucepan, combine the raisins, dried sour cherries, dried cranberries, and vinegar, bring to a boil over high heat, and then drain.

In a bowl, combine the cubed pumpkin, rehydrated dried fruit, onions, and pumpkin seeds and stir to mix well.

Divide the Camembert into 4 equal portions and shape each portion into a patty. Line up half of the bread slices on a work surface. Top each slice with 1 cheese patty, one-fourth of the chutney, and a drizzle of pumpkin seed oil. Close the sandwiches with the remaining bread slices.

Line a large platter with paper towels. In a skillet over high heat, melt 1 tablespoon of the butter. Turn down the heat to low, add 1 sandwich, and cook, turning once, for 2 to 3 minutes on each side, until browned and crisp on both sides and the cheese is melted. Transfer to the prepared platter to blot the excess grease. Repeat with the remaining butter and sandwiches.

Cut the sandwiches in half, plate, and serve.

Horseradish is one of my favorite ingredients. When it gets into your nose, the heat is not overwhelming but rather a visceral spiciness that is unique and powerful. I can think of nothing horseradish pairs with better than beef and beets, making it the perfect bridge to bring the ingredients of this sandwich together. The Brie provides a funk and creaminess that balances the sweetness of the onions and the beets, creating an intensity and harmony of flavors that makes me smile.

prime time

To make the roast beef, preheat the oven to 350°F. Coat the beef with ½ cup of the oil, then season liberally with salt. In a bowl, toss the onions with the remaining ½ cup of oil, then spread the onions on the bottom of a roasting pan. Pour the wine evenly over the onions. Set a wire rack in the pan and place the roast on it.

Roast for about 2 hours, until an instant-read thermometer inserted into the center of the roast away from the bone registers 140°F. Remove from the oven, let cool, thinly slice, and set aside. Transfer the onions to a saucepan and continue to cook over low heat, stirring occasionally, for 10 to 15 minutes, until caramelized, then set aside.

Meanwhile, to make the mayonnaise, wrap the beet in aluminum foil and place in the oven along with the beef. Roast for about 1 hour, until tender when pierced with a knife. Unwrap and, while

CONTINUED >

12 ounces Brie cheese, rind removed

8 slices sourdough bread

ROAST BEEF

1 (2-pound) prime-rib beef roast

1 cup canola oil

1 tablespoon kosher salt

2 white onions, thinly sliced

⅓ cup dry white wine

BEET-HORSERADISH MAYONNAISE

1 red beet

½ cup mayonnaise

6 tablespoons prepared horseradish

1 golden or Chioggia beet

4 tablespoons unsalted butter, for finishing

still hot, rub with a paper towel to peel away the skin. Cut the beet into large dice and let cool.

In a blender, combine the mayonnaise, horseradish, and cooled beet and process for about 3 minutes, until smooth.

Peel the golden beet and cut it into quarters through the stem end. Using a mandoline or a Japanese vegetable slicer, cut the quarters into paper-thin slices (16 to 20 slices total). Divide the Brie into 4 equal portions (3 ounces each) and shape each portion into a patty.

Line up half of the bread slices on a work surface. Spread each slice with a liberal coating of the mayonnaise, then top with a Brie patty, one-fourth of the onions, and 2 or 3 slices of the beef (3 ounces), and finish with 4 or 5 beet slices. Close the sandwiches with the remaining bread slices.

Line a large platter with paper towels. In a skillet over high heat, melt 1 tablespoon of the butter. Turn down the heat to low, add 1 sandwich, and cook, turning once, for 2 to 3 minutes on each side, until browned and crisp on both sides and the cheese is melted. Transfer to the prepared platter to blot the excess grease. Repeat with the remaining butter and sandwiches.

Cut the sandwiches in half, plate, and serve.

spreads and sauces

The addition of a unique spread can turn an ordinary grilled cheese into a great sandwich. This book is filled with spreads that intensify flavors and bring balance to what can otherwise be a very rich affair. They also work as tasty dips for vegetables, fries, or chicken strips and can be used as a base for interesting salad dressings. Like pickles and jams, they can be made ahead and in bulk and will usually keep for up to two weeks in the refrigerator.

Mayonnaise is one of my favorite spreads in a grilled cheese. It adds both a creaminess and another element of flavor. I love to jazz it up with capers, mustards, lemon juice, or horseradish, giving it some punch to cut through the cheese.

Relishes are another welcome addition to a great grilled cheese, contributing not only flavor but also texture and brightness. Mixing something sweet, like roast pumpkin or sweet pickles, with something bright, like lemon juice or vinegar, is a perfect start to a great relish. Then mixing in some fresh herbs and some nuts, seeds, or raw onion for crunch will round out the relish to create a memorable complementary condiment.

Tapenades and chutneys are an ideal balance for even the richest grilled cheese. I love to mix something briny, like capers or olives, with dried fruit, like apricots or raisins, and blend them until they are smooth. Add a little vinegar for brightness and olive oil for a luxurious smoothness and you've got a spread that will elevate a good grilled cheese to star status.

My love affair with the sandwich began when I had my first Monte Cristo at the Bennigan's across the street from the mall. I was ten years old. The fact that the sandwich was dipped in French toast batter, deep-fried, and dusted with confectioners' sugar(!) made me realize just how far a sandwich could go.

The Morning Monte is my ode to that first love. It always seemed that the French toast should be paired with a more breakfasty meat, so I swapped the turkey and ham for fried chicken and bacon. I take the cheese up a notch with Red Hawk triple cream from Cowgirl Creamery in Point Reyes Station, California, though a Brie or Camembert can be substituted, and I make my own strawberry jam. This grilled cheese captures the essence of what I believe to be sandwich royalty.

morning monte

To make the jam, in a small saucepan, combine the berries and granulated sugar, place over low heat, and cook, stirring occasionally, for about 1 hour, until the strawberries break down and the liquid they release is reduced by half. Let cool.

To make the fried chicken, pour the oil to a depth of 2 to 3 inches into a heavy saucepan or deep sauté pan and heat to 350°F on a deep-frying thermometer. Line a large platter with paper towels.

While the oil heats, in a small, shallow bowl, stir together the flour, cayenne pepper, salt, black pepper, and mustard powder.

CONTINUED >

1 pound Cowgirl Creamery Red Hawk triple-cream cheese, rind removed

8 slices white bread

STRAWBERRY JAM

1½ pints fresh strawberries, hulled and halved

2 cups granulated sugar

FRIED CHICKEN

½ gallon canola oil, for deep-frying

1 cup all-purpose flour

1 teaspoon cayenne pepper

1 teaspoon kosher salt

1 teaspoon freshly ground black pepper

1 teaspoon mustard powder

4 chicken tenders (about 1 ounce each)

2 cups buttermilk

12 slices of good quality bacon

>>

In a medium bowl, combine the chicken tenders and buttermilk and stir to coat evenly. Remove the tenders, letting any excess buttermilk drip back into the bowl, and then dredge them in the flour mixture.

When the oil is ready, working in batches to avoid crowding, lift the tenders one at a time from the flour mixture and slide them into the hot oil. Fry for 4 to 6 minutes, until crisp. Using tongs, transfer to the prepared platter to drain.

To cook the bacon, preheat the oven to 350°F. Place a large wire rack on a sheet pan. Line a large platter with paper towels. Arrange the bacon slices, well spaced, on the rack. Place in the oven for 15 to 20 minutes, until crisp. Transfer the bacon to the prepared platter to drain.

To make the French toast batter, in a bowl, whisk together the eggs, cream, milk, vanilla, and granulated sugar until well blended. Pour the egg mixture into a small baking dish. In a large skillet, melt 1 tablespoon of the butter over high heat. Slip a slice of bread into the batter, let soak for soak for 1 minute, then transfer to the skillet. Lower the heat to medium and cook, turning once, for about 3 minutes on each side, until lightly browned and crisp on both sides. Transfer to a large platter. Repeat with the remaining butter and bread slices.

Divide the cheese into 8 equal portions (2 ounces each) and shape each portion into a patty. Line up half of the French toast slices on a work surface. Top each slice with 1 cheese patty, 3 bacon slices, and 1 chicken tender, cut in half on the diagonal, then top with a second cheese patty. Close the sandwiches with the remaining French toast slices.

FRENCH TOAST BATTER

6 eggs

½ cup heavy cream

½ cup whole milk

¼ teaspoon pure vanilla extract

1 teaspoon granulated sugar

4 tablespoons unsalted butter

4 tablespoons unsalted butter, for finishing

1 tablespoon confectioners' sugar

Line a large platter with paper towels. In a skillet over high heat, melt 1 tablespoon of the butter. Turn down the heat to low, add 1 sandwich, and cook, turning once, for 2 to 3 minutes on each side, until browned and crisp on both sides and the cheese is melted. Transfer to the prepared platter to blot the excess grease. Repeat with the remaining butter and sandwiches.

Cut the sandwiches into quarters, dust with confectioners' sugar, plate, and serve. Pass the strawberry jam at the table.

When I opened The Foundry on Melrose in 2007, I wanted to do an accessible yet sophisticated restaurant that anyone could enjoy, a gateway drug to fine dining. When my manager suggested a cheese platter for our bar menu, I felt it sounded too fancy schmancy. But everybody loves grilled cheese, right? So I took the stinky cheese, raisin-walnut bread, dried fruit, and other accoutrements from a cheese plate and made a grilled cheese out of them, then added the short-rib scraps for a more robust experience. It was a hit! The following year we entered the Grilled Cheese Invitational, which is like a mix between Burning Man and a cooking competition, and won. Next, it was featured on Food Network's *The Best Thing I Ever Ate* and in the *New York Times*. Now it's one of the most popular things I serve.

the champ

To make the short ribs, cut the meat into 4 equal chunks and season with salt. In a pressure cooker, combine the meat and stock, lock the lid in place, bring to full pressure, and cook for 45 minutes to an hour, until fork-tender. If you don't have a pressure cooker, combine the seasoned meat and stock in a small, heavy saucepan on the stove top, bring to a boil over high heat, cover, turn down the heat to a gentle simmer, and cook for about 3½ hours, until fork-tender. Transfer the meat to a plate, shred with 2 forks, then return the meat to the cooking liquid to keep it moist.

CONTINUED >

12 ounces Taleggio cheese, rind removed

8 slices dark raisin-walnut bread

SHORT RIBS

8 ounces boneless beef short ribs

1 tablespoon kosher salt

1 cup beef stock

APRICOT-CAPER SPREAD

15 dried apricots

1 tablespoon nonpareil capers

1 tablespoon Dijon mustard

1 tablespoon extra-virgin olive oil

20 dry-packed sun-dried tomatoes

4 small handfuls arugula

4 tablespoons unsalted butter, for finishing

To make the spread, in a small saucepan, combine the apricots with water just to cover, bring to a boil over high heat, and boil for just a few minutes, until fully rehydrated and tender. Drain well and let cool. In a blender, combine the rehydrated apricots, capers, mustard, and oil and process until smooth.

In a small saucepan, combine the sun-dried tomatoes with water just to cover, bring to a boil over high heat, and boil for just a few minutes, until rehydrated and tender. Drain well.

Line up half of the bread slices on a work surface. On each slice, spread 1 tablespoon of the apricot spread, then top with a handful of arugula. Cut the Taleggio into 4 equal portions and gently shape each portion into a patty. Add one cheese patty and one-fourth of the tomatoes and beef to each slice of bread. Close the sandwiches with the remaining bread slices.

Line a large platter with paper towels. In a skillet over high heat, melt 1 tablespoon of the butter. Turn down the heat to low, add 1 sandwich, and cook, turning once, for 2 to 3 minutes on each side, until browned and crisp on both sides and the cheese is melted. Transfer to the prepared platter to blot the excess grease. Repeat with the remaining butter and sandwiches.

Cut the sandwiches in half, plate, and serve.

The idea for this grilled cheese started with one of my favorite flavor combinations, cherries and pistachios. As the inspiration for a sour cherry marmalade started to take shape, the idea hit me to use Manischewitz cherry wine. As a kid at the family table during Shabbat and Passover, this wine was hardly palatable, but it lends the perfect sweetness and cherry note to the marmalade, so I had to include it. Continuing with the Shabbat theme, the use of Manischewitz quickly led me to my bread choice, challah. With a bread so sweet, a cherry marmalade teetering on sour, and a pronounced nuttiness from the pistachios, no other cheese but a good creamy Camembert would do.

cherry cheese ball

To make the marmalade, in a heavy saucepan, combine all of the ingredients, bring to a simmer over high heat, and cook for 10 to 15 minutes, until the liquid is reduced by two-thirds. Transfer to a food processor, let cool slightly, then pulse until a coarse puree forms. Let cool completely.

To prepare the pistachios, preheat the oven to 400°F. In a bowl, toss the pistachios with the oil, sugar, and salt, coating evenly. Spread the nuts on a sheet pan and toast in the oven for 7 to 10 minutes, until fragrant and lightly browned. Pour onto a cutting board, let cool, and coarsely chop.

CONTINUED >

12 ounces Camembert cheese, rind removed

8 slices challah bread

SOUR CHERRY MARMALADE

2 pounds dried sour cherries

1 (750 ml) bottle Manischewitz cherry wine

½ cup red wine vinegar

PISTACHIOS

8 ounces shelled pistachios (1¾ cups)

2 tablespoons olive oil

1½ teaspoons sugar

1½ teaspoons kosher salt

4 tablespoons unsalted butter, for finishing

CHERRY CHEESE BALL, CONTINUED >

Divide the Camembert into 4 equal portions and shape each portion into a patty. Line up half of the bread slices on a work surface. Spread ¼ cup of the marmalade on each slice, then top with 1 cheese patty and sprinkle liberally with the pistachios. Close the sandwiches with the remaining bread slices.

Line a large platter with paper towels. In a skillet over high heat, melt 1 tablespoon of the butter. Turn down the heat to low, add 1 sandwich, and cook, turning once, for 2 to 3 minutes on each side, until browned and crisp on both sides and the cheese is melted. Transfer to the prepared platter to blot the excess grease. Repeat with the remaining butter and sandwiches.

Cut the sandwiches in half, plate, and serve.

06.
gouda, gruyère, and swiss

THE BOOM

*Gouda on olive bread with mushroom-onion ragout
and homemade Worcestershire sauce (V)*...90

THE GOBBLER

*Gouda on pumpernickel with cranberry olive tapenade,
roast turkey, green beans, and fried shallots (M)*..................................91

THE CUBAN REUBEN

*Gruyère on rye with pulled pork, red cabbage kraut,
pickles, and orange-mustard sauce (M)*...95

CHICAGO STYLE

*Swiss on poppy-seed bread with hot dog, giardiniera,
banana pepper and sweet pickle relish, and tomato (M)*..............99

REDBERRY CRUNCH

*Gouda on brioche with raspberry chutney and
pecan brittle (V, S)*...101

This grilled cheese is as meaty a vegetarian sandwich as you can get. The mushroom-onion ragout provides both texture and umami that will make you forget there is no meat. And I had to include a recipe for a vegan Worcestershire, of course. If you're going to do it, do it all the way.

the boom

To make the Worcestershire sauce, combine all of the ingredients in a small saucepan and bring to a boil over high heat. Turn down the heat to a simmer and cook for about 20 minutes, until reduced by half. Let cool.

To make the ragout, in a sauté pan, melt the butter over high heat. As it browns, add the mushrooms and sauté just until they begin to wilt. Add the onion and continue to cook, stirring often, for 10 to 15 minutes, until the onion is tender and caramelized. Add ½ cup of the Worcestershire sauce and continue to cook, stirring, for 5 to 7 minutes, until the vegetables are glazed and all of the liquid has evaporated. Let cool.

Line up half of the bread slices on a work surface. Top each slice with 1 cheese slice, one-fourth of the ragout, and a second slice of cheese. Close the sandwiches with the remaining bread slices.

Line a large platter with paper towels. In a skillet over high heat, melt 1 tablespoon of the butter. Turn down the heat to low, add 1 sandwich, and cook for 2 to 3 minutes on each side, until browned and crisp and the cheese is melted. Transfer to the prepared platter. Repeat with the remaining butter and sandwiches.

Cut the sandwiches in half, plate, and serve.

12 ounces Gouda cheese, cut into 8 equal slices or grated

8 slices olive bread

WORCESTERSHIRE SAUCE

1 cup cider vinegar

¼ cup soy sauce

1 clove garlic, crushed

2 tablespoons brown sugar

½ teaspoon ground ginger

½ teaspoon ground cinnamon

½ teaspoon mustard powder

½ teaspoon freshly ground black pepper

1 whole clove

MUSHROOM-ONION RAGOUT

4 tablespoons unsalted butter

8 ounces shiitake mushrooms, stemmed and sliced

1 yellow onion, thinly sliced

4 tablespoons unsalted butter, for finishing

Thanksgiving is my favorite holiday of the year. It is a celebration of delicious, bountiful food peppered with football and naps—hands-down the best day of the year. Not to mention leftovers that last at least a couple of more days!

The Gobbler is a great way to use your Thanksgiving leftovers. You can substitute cranberry sauce for the tapenade and day-old green bean casserole for the fried shallots and green beans. But what makes this recipe great is that it gives you the opportunity to celebrate Thanksgiving year-round. Thanks for that? You're welcome.

the gobbler

To make the tapenade, in a small saucepan, combine the cranberries and cranberry juice and bring to a boil over high heat. Turn down the heat to a simmer and cook for about 30 minutes, until the cranberries begin to fall apart. Let cool slightly, then transfer to a blender. Add the olives, capers, garlic, and oil and process until smooth.

To make the fried shallots, pour the oil to a depth of 1 to 2 inches into a heavy saucepan or deep sauté pan and heat to 350°F on a deep-frying thermometer. Line a plate with paper towels.

While the oil heats, pour the buttermilk into a small bowl. In a second small bowl, stir together the flour, paprika, chili powder, and black pepper. When the oil is ready, working in batches to avoid crowding, dip the shallot slices in the buttermilk, allowing the excess to drain back into the bowl, and then dredge them in the flour mixture, shaking off the excess. Slide the shallots into

CONTINUED >

12 ounces Gouda cheese, cut into 8 equal slices or grated

8 slices pumpernickel bread

CRANBERRY OLIVE TAPENADE

1 pound fresh cranberries

1 cup cranberry juice

1 cup pitted Niçoise or other brine-cured olives

¼ cup capers

2 cloves garlic, coarsely chopped

½ cup olive oil

FRIED SHALLOTS

½ gallon canola oil, for deep-frying

1 cup buttermilk

1 cup all-purpose flour

1 teaspoon paprika

1 teaspoon chili powder

1teaspoon freshly ground black pepper

8 shallots, thinly sliced

8 ounces green beans, trimmed

12 ounces roasted turkey, leftover or store-bought, cut into 4 thick slices

4 tablespoons unsalted butter, for finishing

the hot oil and fry for 2 to 3 minutes, until golden brown and crisp. Using a slotted spoon, transfer to the prepared plate to drain. Repeat with the remaining shallots.

Fill a large bowl half or two-thirds full with ice cubes and add water to cover. Bring a large pot of salted water to a boil over high heat, add the green beans, and cook for about 3 minutes, until just tender. Drain and immerse in the ice bath for a minute or so, until cold, then drain and blot dry with a kitchen towel.

Line up half of the bread slices on a work surface. Spread each slice with 1 tablespoon of the tapenade, then top with 1 cheese slice, one-fourth each of the turkey, green beans, and shallots, and a second cheese slice. Close the sandwiches with the remaining bread slices.

Line a large platter with paper towels. In a skillet over high heat, melt 1 tablespoon of the butter. Turn down the heat to low, add 1 sandwich, and cook, turning once, for 2 to 3 minutes on each side, until browned and crisp on both sides and the cheese is melted. Transfer to the prepared platter to blot the excess grease. Repeat with the remaining butter and sandwiches.

Cut the sandwiches in half, plate, and serve.

I first met Alfonso Ramirez when I was a line cook at Patina Restaurant in Los Angeles. I loved his work ethic and passion for cooking. We became great friends, and he has continued to be a supportive friend and ally throughout my career. When I returned to Patina as executive chef, he quit Spago to join my team; when I opened Meson G, he became my sous chef; and when I opened The Foundry on Melrose, he was my chef.

Not surprisingly, when the time came to collaborate on a grilled cheese, The Cuban Reuben—a marriage of Alfonso's Cuban roots and my Jewish upbringing—was born. It was a crowd favorite for the entire run of The Foundry.

the cuban reuben

To make the pork, rub the pieces with the mustard, coating them evenly, and then with the garlic, again coating evenly. In a saucepan, melt the manteca over medium heat. Add the pork and sear, turning as needed, for 8 to 10 minutes, until browned on all sides. (You may need to brown the meat in batches to avoid crowding.) Add the orange juice, bring to a simmer, and simmer gently, uncovered, for about 1½ hours, until tender.

Remove from the heat and, using a slotted spoon, transfer the pork to a plate. Continue to simmer the cooking liquid until it is reduced to a glaze consistency. When the pork is cool enough to handle, using 2 forks or your fingers, shred it, transfer it to a heatproof bowl, and pour the reduced cooking liquid over the meat.

CONTINUED >

12 ounces Gruyère cheese, cut into 8 equal slices or grated

8 slices rye bread

PORK

2 pounds pork butt, cut into fist-size chunks

1 cup Dijon mustard

½ cup minced garlic

1 cup manteca (lard)

2 cups fresh orange juice

RED CABBAGE KRAUT

2 cups red wine vinegar

½ cup honey

¼ cup kosher salt

1 head red cabbage, cored and shredded

ORANGE SAUCE

2 cups fresh orange juice

½ cup mayonnaise

½ cup Dijon mustard

Grated zest of 1 orange

2 dill pickles, thinly sliced lengthwise (12 to 16 slices)

4 tablespoons unsalted butter, for finishing

To make the kraut, in a small saucepan, combine the vinegar, honey, and salt and bring to a boil over medium-high heat. Meanwhile, put the cabbage in a heatproof bowl or other container. When the liquid is boiling, remove from the heat, pour over the cabbage, and stir and toss to coat evenly. Let cool in the liquid.

To make the orange sauce, in a small saucepan, bring the orange juice to a boil over high heat and then simmer for about 20 minutes, until reduced to a syrupy consistency. Let cool and transfer to a blender. Add the mayonnaise and mustard and process until smooth. Transfer to a small bowl and fold in the orange zest.

Line up half of the bread slices on a work surface. Spread each slice with 1 tablespoon of the orange sauce, then top with 1 cheese slice, one-fourth of the pork, a small mound of the kraut, 3 or 4 pickle slices, and a second cheese slice. Close the sandwiches with the remaining bread slices.

Line a large platter with paper towels. In a skillet over high heat, melt 1 tablespoon of the butter. Turn down the heat to low, add 1 sandwich, and cook, turning once, for 2 to 3 minutes on each side, until browned and crisp on both sides and the cheese is melted. Transfer to the prepared platter to blot the excess grease. Repeat with the remaining butter and sandwiches.

Cut the sandwiches in half, plate, and serve.

pickles

The sharp acidity and the crunch of a nearly raw vegetable in a sandwich are key to creating intrigue and sophistication. Pickles are important to any balanced sandwich, but they play an even bigger role in a grilled cheese. The salt and vinegar that are the backbone of a great pickled vegetable are the perfect foil for the rich fattiness of both melted cheese and bread crisped in butter.

The success of a pickled vegetable depends on the balance of salt, sugar, and vinegar. Typically, two parts salt and one part sugar is a good formula, but feel free to change this ratio to taste. Although distilled white vinegar is standard, I always enjoy playing around with my choices. Cider vinegar and red wine vinegar are interesting departures, but don't be afraid to get wild with balsamic, sherry, or even raspberry vinegar.

A good pickle is also about the texture of the vegetable. It is important not to overcook your vegetables. They need that crunch and hint of freshness to put their best foot forward. To accomplish this, I recommend bringing your vinegar (with salt, sugar, and any other spices you desire) to a boil and then pour it hot over cut raw vegetables. Once the liquid cools, your pickles are ready. The longer they sit, the better they are, so make them ahead of time if you can. And by all means, make them in bulk. A pickle by its very nature is preserved. Take advantage of that and stockpile these babies for a rainy day and a great grilled cheese sandwich.

Whenever I travel to Chicago, I can't even get out of the airport before hitting up Gold Coast Dogs. The old-fashioned Chicago-style hot dog with neon green relish, the vinegary glory of a *giardiniera*, the heat of a banana pepper, fresh tomato, and poppy-seed bun—not to mention the snap of a good hot dog—lures me every time. Well, this grilled cheese has all of that and more—in this case, cheese. This one is for you, Second City!

chicago style

To make the giardiniera, combine all of the ingredients in a saucepan and bring to a boil over high heat, stirring to dissolve the salt. Transfer to a heatproof bowl, let cool, and then let marinate in the liquid until serving. (The giardiniera will keep in an airtight container in the refrigerator for up to 1 week.)

To make the relish, combine all of the ingredients in a food processor and pulse until chunky.

To cook the hot dogs, in a saucepan, combine the beer and hot dogs and bring to a boil over high heat. Remove from the heat and let the hot dogs cool in the beer. On a charcoal or gas grill or a stove-top grill pan, sear the hot dogs over high heat, turning as needed, until lightly charred.

Line up half of the bread slices on a work surface. Top each slice with 1 cheese slice, 3 tablespoons pickle relish, ½ hot dog (2 pieces), ¼ cup drained giardiniera, 2 tomato slices, and a

CONTINUED >

12 ounces Swiss cheese, cut into 8 equal slices or grated

8 slices poppy-seed bread

GIARDINIERA

2 carrots, peeled and cut into small dice

½ head cauliflower, cut into tiny florets

1 celery stalk, cut into small dice

1 red bell pepper, seeded and cut into small dice

3 oregano sprigs

2 cloves garlic, crushed

½ cup water

½ cup distilled white vinegar

¼ cup kosher salt

2 cups olive oil

BANANA PEPPER AND SWEET PICKLE RELISH

10 banana peppers, stemmed and chopped

½ cup chopped sweet dill pickles

2 shallots, minced

¼ cup sugar

¼ cup cider vinegar

2 drops blue food coloring (if neon green is your desired look!)

>>

second cheese slice. Close the sandwiches with the remaining bread slices.

Line a large platter with paper towels. In a skillet over high heat, melt 1 tablespoon of the butter. Turn down the heat to low, add 1 sandwich, and cook, turning once, for 2 to 3 minutes on each side, until browned and crisp on both sides and the cheese is melted. Transfer to the prepared platter to blot the excess grease. Repeat with the remaining butter and sandwiches.

Cut the sandwiches in half, plate, and serve.

HOT DOG

1 (12-ounce) bottle of your favorite beer

2 (8-inch-long) all-beef hot dogs, halved lengthwise and then crosswise

8 tomato slices

4 tablespoons unsalted butter, for finishing

I love to combine the savory richness of Gouda with intensely sweet-and-sour ingredients. The result is like gladiators in a pit, fighting for your tongue's attention. And no one wins but you! In the Redberry Crunch, the chutney is bright, Bright, BRIGHT! And the brittle is sweet, Sweet, SWEET! Put them together with rich, creamy Gouda, and you've got an unforgettable grilled cheese.

redberry crunch

To make the chutney, combine all of the ingredients in a small saucepan and bring to a boil over high heat. Turn down the heat to a simmer and cook, stirring occasionally, for about 30 minutes, until the berries have broken down and all of the liquid has evaporated. Let cool.

To make the brittle, spray a sheet pan with nonstick cooking spray. In a glass bowl, combine the pecans, sugar, corn syrup, and salt and microwave for 3½ minutes. Stir well, then microwave for 3½ minutes longer. Stir in the butter and microwave for 2 minutes longer. Finally, stir in the baking powder until foamy, then pour the mixture out onto the prepared sheet pan and spread in an even layer. Let cool completely, then break the brittle into small bite-size pieces.

Line up half of the bread slices on a work surface. Spread each slice with ¼ cup of the chutney, then top with 2 cheese slices and sprinkle liberally with the brittle. Close the sandwiches with the remaining bread slices.

CONTINUED >

12 ounces Gouda cheese, cut into 8 equal slices or grated

8 slices brioche bread

RASPBERRY CHUTNEY

2 pints fresh raspberries

½ cup raspberry vinegar or red wine vinegar

¼ cup sugar

PECAN BRITTLE

1 cup chopped pecans

1 cup sugar

½ cup light corn syrup

⅛ teaspoon kosher salt

1 tablespoon unsalted butter

1 teaspoon baking soda

4 tablespoons unsalted butter, for finishing

Line a large platter with paper towels. In a skillet over high heat, melt 1 tablespoon of the butter. Turn down the heat to low, add 1 sandwich, and cook, turning once, for 2 to 3 minutes on each side, until browned and crisp on both sides and the cheese is melted. Transfer to the prepared platter to blot the excess grease. Repeat with the remaining butter and sandwiches.

Cut the sandwiches in half, plate, and serve.

07.
goat

BEET IT
Goat cheese on rye with beets four ways: red beet puree, roasted golden beets, beet greens, and Chioggia beet slices (V) 107

LOX OF LOVE
Goat cheese on rye with smoked salmon, pickled cucumber and red onion, and caper-dill spread (B, M) 109

WINTER WONDERLAND
Goat cheese on sourdough with chestnuts, roasted celery root and sage, and bourbon-glazed ham (M) 112

ELVIS
Goat cheese on white bread with peanut butter, banana, and bacon (M, S) 117

MONTMARTRE
Goat cheese on brioche with fig marmalade and lavender honey (B, V, S) 119

One of my favorite ingredients is beets. In addition to being earthy and sweet, they are also colorful. Here, ruby red beet puree, golden yellow roasted beets, and a swirly red-and-white raw Chioggia make for a beautiful grilled cheese. It seems like nearly every restaurant in America has a salad of goat cheese and beets, so I figured why not combine them in a sandwich? The seeds in the rye bread bring a great nuttiness and crunch that add even more texture to an already textured dish.

beet it

To make the beet puree, preheat the oven to 350°F. Wrap the red beet in aluminum foil and roast for about 1 hour, until tender when pierced with a knife. Unwrap and, while still hot, rub with a paper towel to peel away the skin. Cut the beet into large dice, let cool, transfer to a blender, add the vinegar and oil, and process until smooth. Leave the oven on for the golden beets.

To roast the golden beets, cut off the beet tops, chop, and set them aside. In a bowl, toss the beets with 2 tablespoons of the oil, coating evenly, then spread them in a single layer on a sheet pan. Roast for 30 to 40 minutes, until tender when pierced with a knife. While still hot, rub with paper towels to peel away the skin. Cut the beets into quarters through the stem end and transfer to a bowl.

In a sauté pan, heat the remaining 2 tablespoons oil over high heat. Add the beet greens and cook, stirring, for 3 to 5 minutes, just until wilted. Transfer to the bowl with the beets and toss until well mixed. Let cool.

CONTINUED >

**12 ounces fresh
goat cheese**

8 slices rye bread

BALSAMIC BEET PUREE

1 red beet

¼ cup balsamic vinegar

¼ cup olive oil

ROASTED
GOLDEN BEETS

1 bunch baby golden beets, with tops

4 tablespoons olive oil

1 Chioggia beet, peeled and thinly sliced (8 slices)

4 tablespoons unsalted butter, for finishing

Line up half of the bread slices on a work surface. Spread 1 tablespoon of the beet puree on each slice, top with one-fourth of the cheese and then one-fourth of the golden beets and greens, and finish with 2 Chioggia beet slices. Close the sandwiches with the remaining bread slices.

Line a large platter with paper towels. In a skillet over high heat, melt 1 tablespoon of the butter. Turn down the heat to low, add 1 sandwich, and cook, turning once, for 2 to 3 minutes on each side, until browned and crisp on both sides and the cheese is melted. Transfer to the prepared platter to blot the excess grease. Repeat with the remaining butter and sandwiches.

Cut the sandwiches in half, plate, and serve.

Being raised Jewish in America, I know my way around a bagel and lox. That combo is one of my dearest childhood memories. Here I combine that pair with grilled cheese, marrying two childhood favorites into one. In Lox of Love, I use goat cheese instead of cream cheese because I like the extra richness and tang, but cream cheese would work as well. The pickled vegetables, which draw on the traditional accompaniments of a classic bagel sandwich, deliver the bite needed to temper the richness and saltiness of this sandwich.

lox of love

To make the pickled vegetables, put the cucumbers and onion in a heatproof bowl. In a small saucepan, combine the vinegar, sugar, and salt and bring to a boil over high heat. Remove from the heat, pour over the vegetables, and let cool. Drain the vegetables before using.

To make the spread, in a blender, combine the lemon juice, capers, dill, mustard, and egg yolk and process on low speed just until smooth. With the blender running, add the oil in a slow, thin stream and process until a mayonnaise-like consistency forms.

Line up half of the bread slices on a work surface. Spread one-fourth of the cheese on each slice, then top with one-fourth each of the caper-dill spread, the salmon, and the pickled vegetables. Close the sandwiches with the remaining bread slices.

CONTINUED >

12 ounces fresh goat cheese

8 slices rye bread

PICKLED VEGETABLES

2 Persian cucumbers, thinly sliced

1 red onion, thinly sliced

½ cup red wine vinegar

1½ teaspoons sugar

1½ teaspoons kosher salt

CAPER-DILL SPREAD

Juice of 1 lemon

1 tablespoon nonpareil capers

1 tablespoon chopped fresh dill

1 tablespoon Dijon mustard

1 egg yolk

½ cup olive oil

8 ounces thinly sliced smoked salmon

4 tablespoons unsalted butter, for finishing

LOX OF LOVE, CONTINUED >

Line a large platter with paper towels. In a skillet over high heat, melt 1 tablespoon of the butter. Turn down the heat to low, add 1 sandwich, and cook, turning once, for 2 to 3 minutes on each side, until browned and crisp on both sides and the cheese is melted. Transfer to the prepared platter to blot the excess grease. Repeat with the remaining butter and sandwiches.

Cut the sandwiches in half, plate, and serve.

Here is one of my favorite winter sandwiches. Root vegetables fill the farmers' market, Christmas songs are playing on the radio—"Chestnuts roasting on an open fire..."—and every night feels like the perfect night for a bourbon. I've found that O'Banon goat cheese from Capriole dairy in Greenville, Indiana, was made for this sandwich. It's a soft cheese wrapped in chestnut leaves and then soaked in bourbon—and it tastes even better than it sounds. It has won too many awards to list here and is one of the finest American-made cheeses available. (If O'Banon is out of your reach, use the best soft goat cheese you can find.) This deliciously acidic cheese and the sourdough bread complement the sweet smokiness of the glazed ham perfectly, while the sage, chestnuts, and celery root contribute a deep earthiness to this seasonal masterpiece.

winter wonderland

To roast the chestnuts, preheat the oven to 400°F. Using a small, sharp knife, cut an X through the skin (about ⅛ inch deep) on the rounded side of each chestnut. Lay the chestnuts, flat sides down, on a sheet pan. Roast for about 30 minutes, until the edges of the skin curl back and the chestnuts are tender when pierced with the knife. When the chestnuts are just cool enough to handle, peel away the shells and tough inner skin. Set aside to cool. Cut the chestnuts in half. Leave the oven on for the celery root.

To prepare the celery root, in a bowl, toss together the celery root, sage, and butter, coating evenly. Spread the mixture in a single layer on a sheet pan and roast for 7 to 10 minutes, until lightly colored and tender when pierced with a knife. Let cool.

2 (6-ounce) wheels Capriole O'Banon goat cheese

8 slices sourdough bread

CHESTNUTS

1 pound chestnuts

CELERY ROOT

2 celery roots, peeled and diced

Leaves from 1 bunch sage, cut into chiffonade

4 tablespoons unsalted butter, melted

BOURBON-GLAZED HAM

1 (750 ml) bottle bourbon

8 ounces good-quality country ham, cut into 4 equal slices

4 tablespoons unsalted butter, for finishing

To make the ham, reduce the oven to 325°F. Pour the bourbon into a small saucepan, bring to a boil over high heat and boil for 15 to 20 minutes, until reduced to a syrupy consistency. Let cool to room temperature. Place a large wire rack on a sheet pan, arrange the ham slices in a single layer on the rack, and then brush the ham liberally on both sides with the glaze. Place in the oven and cook until the ham is lightly caramelized, 7 to 10 minutes. Let cool.

Line up half of the bread slices on a work surface. Crumble ½ wheel of the cheese over each slice, then top with 1 ham slice, one-fourth of the chestnuts (about 7 nuts in total), and one-fourth of the celery root. Close the sandwiches with the remaining bread slices.

Line a large platter with paper towels. In a skillet over high heat, melt 1 tablespoon of the butter. Turn down the heat to low, add 1 sandwich, and cook, turning once, for 2 to 3 minutes on each side, until browned and crisp on both sides and the cheese is melted. Transfer to the prepared platter to blot the excess grease. Repeat with the remaining butter and sandwiches.

Cut the sandwiches in half, plate, and serve.

using the sweet stuff

I always like to have fun with my dishes, and my grilled cheeses are no different. One way that I like to mix it up is by combining sweet with savory. Jams are the obvious way to add sweetness, but there are other, unexpected ways to bring sweetness to a great savory grilled cheese.

Glazing meats brings the sweet to the salt. Glazes come in many guises: a balsamic vinegar reduction, melted brown sugar, maple syrup, or even the reduction of a favorite liquor (see page 112). When you apply that glaze to a meat and throw it in a low oven, the meat will candy, and your grilled cheese will get happy, happy.

Candied nuts can also add complexity to a grilled cheese. They bring an earthiness to match the sweetness, which gives depth to any sandwich. And you can take candied nuts to another level. Bake them into a brittle (see page 101) for a more intense sweetness and crunch. Or blend them into a pesto (see page 34) for a special sweet-salt combination.

All hail the king! We regularly had live music—everything from jazz to solo piano to country rock—at my first restaurant, The Foundry on Melrose. But I like to think it was our Halloween performance that was the crowning jewel. Every October 31, I'd don a white onesie with a cape, team up with a rock-and-roll quartet, and belt out six of my favorite Elvis songs. In homage, I felt I had to take the time to turn Elvis Presley's favorite sandwich—peanut butter, banana, and bacon—into a grilled cheese. Here are two of America's great ambassadors combined into many delicious bites!

elvis

Preheat the oven to 350°F. Place a large wire rack on a sheet pan. Line a platter with paper towels. Arrange the bacon slices, well spaced, on the rack. (The bacon will cook up crispier on the rack while the fat collects in the pan. This is key to the bacon remaining crisp in a grilled cheese.) Place in the oven for 15 to 20 minutes, until crisp. Transfer the bacon to the prepared platter to drain. Scoop up 2 tablespoons of the bacon fat from the sheet pan to use for the spread.

To make the spread, in a small saucepan, combine the peanut butter and cheese, place over low heat, and stir just until soft and well mixed. Transfer to a food processor, add the bacon fat, and process until smooth.

CONTINUED >

8 slices white bread

8 slices of good-quality bacon

PEANUT BUTTER SPREAD

½ cup peanut butter

12 ounces fresh goat cheese

2 tablespoons bacon fat, from cooking bacon

2 bananas, peeled and sliced crosswise

4 tablespoons unsalted butter, for finishing

Line up half of the bread slices on a work surface. Slather one-fourth of the spread on each slice, then top with one-fourth of the banana slices and 2 bacon slices. Close the sandwiches with the remaining bread slices.

Line a large platter with paper towels. In a skillet over high heat, melt 1 tablespoon of the butter. Turn down the heat to low, add 1 sandwich, and cook, turning once, for 2 to 3 minutes on each side, until browned and crisp on both sides and the cheese is melted. Transfer to the prepared platter to blot the excess grease. Repeat with the remaining butter and sandwiches.

Cut the sandwiches in half, plate, and serve.

Much of my love for food and my understanding of great ingredients came from my time enrolled at Le Cordon Bleu in Paris, when I would spend my off-hours wandering the streets of the city and sampling the goods at every small *boulangerie* and *fromagerie*. This grilled cheese captures the essence of those days.

Any goat cheese would work for the Montmartre, though I think a firm, aged goat cheese is preferred. The age allows for more depth of flavor to stand up to the other ingredients. The perfect pairing is one of the most original-tasting American-made cheeses I've encountered: Barely Buzzed from the Beehive Cheese Company in Uintah, Utah, which is rubbed with coffee and lavender. The bitter nuttiness of the coffee foils the sweetness of the figs, while the lavender brings out the same notes in the honey. If you are pressed for time, you can purchase lavender honey at specialty food stores and well-stocked supermarkets.

montmartre

To make the marmalade, combine all of the ingredients in a small, heavy saucepan and bring to a boil over medium-high heat, stirring to dissolve the sugar. Turn down the heat to a simmer and cook for 15 to 20 minutes, stirring constantly to prevent scorching. The figs will have broken down and the liquid will have almost fully evaporated. Let cool slightly, transfer to a blender, and process until smooth. Let cool to room temperature.

CONTINUED >

12 ounces Beehive Barely Buzzed goat cheese, cut into 8 equal slices or grated

8 slices brioche bread

FIG MARMALADE

1 pint fresh figs (about 15 to 18), stemmed and halved lengthwise, or 8 ounces dried figs, stemmed

½ cup balsamic vinegar

1 cup water

¼ cup sugar

LAVENDER HONEY

1 cup clover or other mild-flavored honey

Blossoms from 1 bunch pesticide-free fresh lavender, or ¼ cup culinary-grade dried lavender blossoms

4 tablespoons unsalted butter, for finishing

To make the lavender honey, combine the honey and lavender in a small, heavy saucepan, bring to a boil over medium-high heat, and remove from the heat. Let cool, then store in a small jar with a sealable lid.

Line up half of the bread slices on a work surface. Top each slice with 1 cheese slice, then spread the cheese with ¼ cup of the marmalade, drizzle with ½ teaspoon of the honey, and finish with a second cheese slice. Close the sandwiches with the remaining bread slices.

Line a large platter with paper towels. In a skillet over high heat, melt 1 tablespoon of the butter. Turn down the heat to low, add 1 sandwich, and cook, turning once, for 2 to 3 minutes on each side, until browned and crisp on both sides and the cheese is melted. Transfer to the prepared platter to blot the excess grease. Repeat with the remaining butter and sandwiches.

Cut the sandwiches in half, plate, and serve.

08.
wild cards

When I was growing up, Muenster frequently made its way into our grilled cheese sandwiches because it was my older brother Jason's favorite cheese. It always seemed like a high-end American processed cheese to me, if there is such a thing, so I've treated it like royalty here. The earthy asparagus—roasted and raw—is the star of this grilled cheese. Caramelized shallots, dubbed the "BMW of onions" by my mentor Joachim Splichal, and bits of fresh thyme further elevate the sandwich. The Top Shelf is an expression of highbrow and lowbrow meeting in the middle for everyone to enjoy.

top shelf

To prepare the asparagus, preheat the oven to 450°F. Pile the pencil-thin asparagus on a sheet pan, drizzle with the oil, toss to coat evenly, then spread in a single layer. Roast for about 10 minutes, until just tender. Transfer to a cutting board and cut into 2-inch lengths.

Trim the woody ends from the jumbo asparagus, then, using a vegetable peeler, lightly peel the lower half of each stalk. Using a mandoline or a Japanese vegetable slicer, thinly slice the spears lengthwise. You should have 16 to 20 ribbons.

To prepare the shallots, in a sauté pan, melt the butter over high heat until it foams and browns slightly. Add the shallots and thyme, turn down the heat to low, and cook, stirring occasionally, for 15 to 20 until translucent and tender. Remove from the heat. Let cool.

CONTINUED >

12 ounces Muenster cheese, cut into 8 equal slices or grated

8 slices potato bread

ASPARAGUS

1 bunch pencil-thin asparagus, about ¾ pound, woody ends trimmed

¼ cup olive oil

3 jumbo asparagus spears

SHALLOTS

4 tablespoons unsalted butter

8 shallots, thinly sliced

1 tablespoon fresh chopped thyme leaves

4 tablespoons unsalted butter, for finishing

Line up half of the bread slices on a work surface. Top each slice with 1 cheese slice, one-fourth of the cooked asparagus, one-fourth of the shallots, 4 or 5 raw asparagus ribbons, and finally a second cheese slice. Close the sandwiches with the remaining bread slices.

Line a large platter with paper towels. In a skillet over high heat, melt 1 tablespoon of the butter. Turn down the heat to low, add 1 sandwich, and cook, turning once, for 2 to 3 minutes on each side, until browned and crisp on both sides and the cheese is melted. Transfer to the prepared platter to blot the excess grease. Repeat with the remaining butter and sandwiches.

Cut the sandwiches in half, plate, and serve.

I live and work in Los Angeles, so Mexican culture constantly inspires my food. Like a grilled cheese, a mole, when done well, shows incredible depth of flavor and attacks all of the tongue's senses. But while most moles take three days to make, this recipe is an easy "cheat" that turns out a great one in a very short time.

The sweet and spice of the mole play off the richness of the chorizo and black beans, and the spicy marinated onions bring all of the flavors together. My favorite Mexican restaurant in Los Angeles, The Garden of Taxco, has a saying: "It's not hot, it's spicy." The Mole Melt lends truth to the saying.

mole melt

To make the chorizo and beans, in a saucepan, heat the canola oil over high heat. When the oil is hot, add the chorizo, turn down the heat to low, and cook, stirring occasionally, for about 10 minutes, until the chorizo has rendered its fat and is cooked through. Add the beans and stir vigorously until the beans break up and are mashed with the chorizo. Remove from the heat.

To make the mayonnaise, in a small saucepan, combine the chocolate, orange juice, peanuts, apricots, raisins, chiles, garlic, cumin, and coriander and bring to a boil over high heat. Boil for 5 to 7 minutes, until the fruit and garlic are tender, the chocolate is fully melted, and the juice has almost fully evaporated. Transfer to a blender, add the mayonnaise, and process until smooth. Let cool.

CONTINUED >

1 pound Cotija cheese, crumbled

8 slices wheat bread

CHORIZO AND BEANS

1 tablespoon canola oil

½ pound Mexican chorizo, casing removed and crumbled

½ cup drained cooked black beans

CHOCOLATE MOLE MAYONNAISE

1 tablet Abuelita brand Mexican hot chocolate

1 cup fresh orange juice

¼ cup roasted peanuts

¼ cup dried apricots

¼ cup golden raisins

4 Fresno chiles, stemmed

2 cloves garlic

½ teaspoon ground cumin, toasted in a dry pan

½ teaspoon coriander seeds, toasted in a dry pan

1 cup mayonnaise

>>

To make the marinated onion, using a mandoline or a Japanese vegetable slicer, cut the onion into paper-thin slices. Put the slices into a small bowl, add the hot sauce and lime juice, toss to mix, and let marinate for 2 hours.

Line up half of the bread slices on a work surface. Spread 2 tablespoons of the mayonnaise on each slice, then top with ¼ cup of the bean-chorizo mixture and one-fourth each of the cheese, marinated onions, and cilantro leaves. Close the sandwiches with the remaining bread slices.

Line a large platter with paper towels. In a skillet over high heat, melt 1 tablespoon of the butter. Turn down the heat to low, add 1 sandwich, and cook, turning once, for 2 to 3 minutes on each side, until browned and crisp on both sides and the cheese is melted. Transfer to the prepared platter to blot the excess grease. Repeat with the remaining butter and sandwiches.

Cut the sandwiches in half, plate, and serve.

MARINATED RED ONIONS

1 red onion, thinly sliced

1 (5-ounce) bottle Tapatío brand or other bottled hot sauce

Juice of 2 limes

Leaves from 1 bunch cilantro

4 tablespoons unsalted butter, for finishing

buying versus making ingredients

I have included a lot of recipes for the ingredients used in this book. You can make your own American cheese (see page 22), poach your own tuna (see page 45), and bake your own cornbread (see page 57). Some of these recipes are too time-consuming to make when all you want is a quick sandwich. I think it's important to have the option to put together everything from scratch, but to know that when time is short, it's all right to buy ingredients.

For example, pickling your own vegetables is fun and you can put up a batch in advance, but great pickled items are available at many grocery stores. It's the bite of the vinegar to cut the fat that's important, so if you can't find the exact ingredient called for in the recipe, play around. Pickled cucumbers can be substituted for alternative styles and flavors of pickle, *giardiniera* is available in many stores, and sauerkraut can be substituted for pickled red cabbage. The same goes for jams. Many great flavors are stocked in grocery stores, so feel free to mix and match as you like.

What's important is that you buy good-quality ingredients. What's more important is that you enjoy your grilled cheese–making experience without being stressed about time or ability.

Few American culinary cultures are more unique than you find in the Hawaiian Islands. The balance of tropical and Asian flavors along with Army rations are all featured in this delicious grilled cheese. Hawaiian bread is a favorite of mine for nearly everything, and here it makes too much sense to omit. Crunchy, sweet pineapple and soy-glazed spiced ham? Pure Hawaii. Finally, the heat and brightness of the relish round this baby out, leaving your taste buds ready to say aloha.

big island

To make the spiced ham, heat a cast-iron skillet over high heat and add the oil. When the oil is hot, add the ham slices and cook, turning once, for about 3 minutes on each side, until crisp and browned. Set aside to cool.

In a small saucepan, combine the soy sauce, pineapple juice, and honey and bring to boil over high heat. Cook for 10 to 15 minutes, until reduced to a syrupy consistency. Add the ham slices and swirl the pan until the slices are evenly glazed and sticky. Remove from the heat.

To make the relish, combine all of the ingredients in a bowl and stir to mix well.

Line up half of the bread slices on a work surface. Top each slice with 1 cheese slice, 1 ham slice, a heaping spoonful of the

CONTINUED >

12 ounces Jack cheese, cut into 8 equal slices or grated

8 slices Hawaiian bread

SPICED HAM

2 tablespoons canola oil

1 (7-ounce) can spiced ham, cut into 4 equal slices

½ cup soy sauce

2 cups pineapple juice

¼ cup honey

PINEAPPLE-JALAPEÑO RELISH

1 jalapeño chile, stemmed and minced

¼ pineapple, peeled, cored, and cut into small dice

1 tomato, cut into small dice

½ red onion, cut into small dice

Leaves from ½ bunch cilantro

¼ cup olive oil

Juice of 1 lime

4 tablespoons unsalted butter, for finishing

relish, and a second cheese slice. Close the sandwiches with the remaining bread slices.

Line a large platter with paper towels. In a skillet over high heat, melt 1 tablespoon of the butter. Turn down the heat to low, add 1 sandwich, and cook, turning once, for 2 to 3 minutes on each side, until browned and crisp on both sides and the cheese is melted. Transfer to the prepared platter to blot the excess grease. Repeat with the remaining butter and sandwiches.

Cut the sandwiches in half, plate, and serve.

Most of us immediately reflect on mom's home kitchen when it comes to our first grilled cheese experience. But chances are you ate your first restaurant grilled cheese in one of the many Greek-run diners in this country, especially if you lived along the Eastern Seaboard. This grilled cheese is an homage to that heritage. The olives in the bread heighten the saltiness of the feta; the lamb, a Greek staple, provides a gaminess to balance the saltiness; and the pomegranate and cucumber in the mint salad bring a unique freshness. And once you enjoy the crunch of fried chickpeas, you'll start adding them to nearly everything you make. I know I do.

the greek

To make the lamb, in a cast-iron or other heavy skillet, heat the oil over high heat. Add the lamb and cook, stirring to break up the meat with a wooden spoon, until it begins to brown. Add the salt, oregano, and mint and continue to cook, stirring occasionally, for about 4 minutes, until the lamb is cooked through. Remove from the heat.

To make the salad, combine all of the ingredients in a bowl and stir to mix well.

To fry the chickpeas, pour the oil to a depth of 1 to 2 inches into a heavy saucepan or deep sauté pan and heat to 350°F on a deep-frying thermometer. Add the chickpeas and fry for about 5 minutes, until browned and crisp. Drain the chickpeas on a plate lined with paper towels. Transfer to a bowl. Sprinkle with the chili powder and salt and toss to coat evenly.

CONTINUED >

12 ounces feta cheese, crumbled

8 slices olive bread

GROUND LAMB

2 tablespoons canola oil

8 ounces ground lamb

Pinch of kosher salt

1 tablespoon chopped fresh oregano

1 tablespoon chopped fresh mint

MINT SALAD

Leaves from 2 bunches mint

½ red onion, thinly sliced

½ cucumber, thinly sliced

½ cup pomegranate seeds

¼ cup fresh lemon juice

¼ cup olive oil

FRIED CHICKPEAS

½ gallon canola oil, for deep-frying

1 cup drained canned chickpeas

Pinch of chili powder

Pinch of kosher salt

4 tablespoon unsalted butter, for finishing

Line up half of the bread slices on a work surface. Top each slice with 2 ounces (about ⅓ cup) of the cheese, one-fourth each of the lamb, salad, and chickpeas, and then finish with another 1 ounce (about 2½ tablespoons) of the cheese. Close the sandwiches with the remaining bread slices.

Line a large platter with paper towels. In a skillet over high heat, melt 1 tablespoon of the butter. Turn down the heat to low, add 1 sandwich, and cook, turning once, for 2 to 3 minutes on each side, until browned and crisp on both sides and the cheese is melted. Transfer to the prepared platter to blot the excess grease. Repeat with the remaining butter and sandwiches.

Cut the sandwiches in half, plate, and serve.

This dessert grilled cheese is an ode to my favorite French combo: Nutella and banana. Here, the heightened acidity of the fromage blanc balances the incredible sweetness of the chocolate-hazelnut spread. I recommend Askinosie brand; it's made from scratch using homemade hazelnut butter prepared with DuChilly hazelnuts, harvested from an orchard in Lynden, Washington, and its "nut to jar" integrity comes shining through. But Nutella is a pretty delicious substitute. And let's not forget the bananas. Soaking them in rum adds a complexity and bite that rounds out this entire sordid affair.

choc-full of nuts

To soak the bananas, in a small bowl, combine the bananas and rum, mixing gently. Let stand for at least 4 hours or preferably up to overnight. Strain.

In a bowl, combine the fromage blanc with the bananas and mix well.

Line up half of the bread slices on a work surface. Spread one-fourth of the chocolate-hazelnut spread on each slice and top with one-fourth of the fromage blanc mixture. Close the sandwiches with the remaining bread slices.

Line a large platter with paper towels. In a skillet over high heat, melt 1 tablespoon of the butter. Turn down the heat to low, add 1 sandwich, and cook, turning once, for 2 to 3 minutes on each side, until browned and crisp on both sides and the cheese is melted. Transfer to the prepared platter to blot the excess grease. Repeat with the remaining butter and sandwiches.

Cut the sandwiches in half, plate, and serve.

12 ounces fromage blanc, at room temperature

8 slices brioche bread

RUM-SOAKED BANANAS

2 bananas, peeled and cut into ¼-inch-thick slices

½ cup dark rum

12 ounces Askinosie brand chocolate-hazelnut spread (generous 1 cup)

4 tablespoons unsalted butter, for finishing

index